T0354547

TOOLS FOR
POLICY
RESEARCH

TOOLS FOR
POLICY
RESEARCH

BONARD MWAPE
AND
JOSEPH MUMBA

authorHOUSE®

AuthorHouse™
1663 Liberty Drive
Bloomington, IN 47403
www.authorhouse.com
Phone: 1-800-839-8640

Published by AuthorHouse   04/05/2012

ISBN: 978-1-4678-9672-6 (sc)
ISBN: 978-1-4678-9673-3 (e)

CONTENTS

CHAPTER ONE

INTRODUCTION
TO POLICY RESEARCH

1.1 WHAT IS POLICY RESEARCH?

There are many approaches to conducting a policy research. You as a student should first understand what your school or university requires. In many schools of business, and at Eastern and Southern African Management Institute (ESAMI) in particular, we require that students collect their own data in addition to any secondary data. This requirement is different from some business schools, where the student uses in his or her thesis only data that has already been collected. If you are not sure about the difference between these two approaches, clarify the situation with your thesis supervisor. Similarly, the term *policy research* is used here to refer to studies made on either a policy, a programme, a project, or a strategy. The student can either do an impact assessment or a historical review of the development of a policy, programme, project, strategy, and so on. It is important to clarify with the school whether your study meets the school's requirement. At ESAMI no study is done before a student's research proposal is approved by the school. After the approval, the school allocates a supervisor to guide the student during the research process.

Policy research in ESAMI is taken to be a systematic and organized effort to investigate a specific problem encountered in any organization.

1

Many theses in ESAMI have been done on the private sector, NGOs, civic societies, and the public sector, or any organizational environment. The research has involved a series of well-planned steps executed with the aim of finding a solution to the problem of concern to the manager in that organization or business environment.

The first step is for the student to identify the research problem. Once the research problem has been approved by the school, the student works with the supervisor to develop a fully-fledged proposal. When it has been approved, data has to be gathered and analysed in order to determine the factors that have a direct or indirect bearing on the problem so that the necessary corrective action can be instituted.

Table 1.1 shows some commonly researched policy topics in the ESAMI MBA program. Table 1.1 can provide a guide to students in identifying research topics for their MBA theses. The topics given in Table 1.1 are not exhaustive; they are only a sample. Appendix 1 shows some examples of past student thesis topics in the ESAMI MBA program.

Table 1.1 Major Topics in Policy Research

Area	Topic
1. Management and Organizational Behaviour	Brand loyalty and product innovation
	Total quality management
	Morale and job satisfaction
	Leadership style
	Employee behaviours, e.g., absenteeism, turnover, performance
	Strategy formulation
	Employee selection, recruitment, and training
	Organizational communication
	Downsizing
	Organizational effectiveness

Table 1.1 (Continued)

2. Finance and Accounting	Cost of capital, valuation of firms, and investment decisions
	Stock, bond, and commodity value predictions
	Risk assessment
	Foreign direct investment
	Tax impacts
	Cost accounting procedures
	Mergers and acquisitions
	Portfolio analysis
	Performance of financial markets
	Capital asset pricing
3. Sales and Marketing	Sales analysis
	Market share
	Market potential
	New product concept
	Advertising
	Buyer behaviour
	Customer complaints and satisfaction
	e-marketing
4. Information Systems	Installation of management information systems
	Knowledge and information needs assessment
	Database systems and analysis
	Customer relationship management systems
	Technical support satisfaction
5. Corporate Responsibility and Green Issues	Environmental impact of business
	Social values and ethics
	Global warming mitigation
	Catchment area management
	HIV/AIDS impacts and strategies
	Sex, age, and worker equity
	Waste management
	Poverty impacts and strategies

Based on past ESAMI executive MBA student dissertations, 1999-2008.

1.2 KEY CONCEPTS, ELEMENTS, AND TYPES OF POLICY RESEARCH

Research can be classified according to the following criteria (Collis and Hussey, 2003):

1. *Purpose* of research. The purpose of research is the reason why you are conducting a given research.
2. *Process* of research. The process of research shows the way in which data will be collected and analysed.
3. *Logic* of research. The logic of research shows whether you are moving from the general to the specific or vice versa.
4. *Outcome* of research. The outcome of research shows whether the outcome is to solve a given problem or the outcome is to generate knowledge.

Table 1.2 shows types of research based on this classification.

Table 1.2 Types of Business Policy Research

Basis of Classification	Type of Research
Purpose of research	Exploratory, descriptive, analytical (explanatory), or predictive research
Process or approach of research	Quantitative or qualitative research
Logic of research	Deductive or inductive research
Outcome of research	Applied or basic research

Based on Collis and Hussey, 2003.

Exploratory research is conducted when there is little or no information about the research problem because there are few or no past research studies. Exploratory research aims to look for patterns, ideas, or hypotheses. It is not aimed at testing hypotheses. Typical research techniques used in exploratory research include case studies, observation, and historical analysis. Both quantitative and qualitative data can be collected in exploratory research.

Descriptive research is conducted to characterize or profile an issue, problem, persons, events, products, objects, or situations as they exist. Descriptive research goes further than exploratory research in examining a problem or issue. Descriptive research aims answering the "what?", "who?", "where?", "when?", and "how?" research questions. Some examples of research questions requiring a descriptive study would be:

1. What are our sales in Lusaka compared to our sales in Blantyre?
2. What has been the level of sales in Nairobi over the last five years?
3. What is the absentee rate in the Executive MBA class?
4. What are the feelings of workers about the impending downsizing?
5. What are the qualifications of accountants in East Africa?

Analytical or explanatory research can be a continuation of descriptive research. Analytical research goes beyond just profiling a problem or situation to explaining or analysing why the problem is occurring. Analytical research aims at answering the "why?" and the "how?" research questions. Examples of research questions requiring analytical research would be:

1. Why have the sales of our products in Dar es Salaam been so high?
2. Why do we have high staff turnover in our Kampala Branch?
3. How can we expand the range of our services in West Africa?
4. How can we reduce the number of complaints made by our customers in the Southern Africa market?

Predictive research can go even further than analytical research. Predictive research forecasts the probability of a similar situation happening elsewhere. Predictive research aims at answering the "will?" and the "how?" research questions. Examples of research questions requiring a predictive study include:

1. Will a change in packaging improve our sales in West Africa?
2. How will an increase in interest rates affect our profit margin in Tanzania?

Classifying research according to the process or approach of research divides research into quantitative and qualitative research.

Quantitative research uses an objective approach. It measures phenomena to produce numerical or quantifiable data that can be rendered to statistical analysis and the testing of hypothesis. *Qualitative research* uses a subjective approach to collect non-numeric data reflecting perceptions of the research subjects in order to gain an understanding of social and human activities.

Deductive research involves developing a conceptual and theoretical structure which is tested by empirical observation (Collis and Hussey, 2003; Gill and Johnson, 1991). Deductive research therefore "tests theory." Deductive research is conducted through the following sequential stages (Saunders *et al.*, 2007):

Developing the theory.

Deducing a hypothesis from the theory.

1. Expressing the hypothesis in operational terms (that is, indicating exactly how the concepts or variables are to be measured), which proposes a relationship between two specific concepts or variables.

2. Testing this operational hypothesis.
3. Examining the specific outcome of the inquiry; this will tend either to confirm the theory or indicate the need to modify it.
4. If necessary, modifying the theory in the light of the findings.

Inductive research involves developing a theory from the observation of empirical reality. Inductive research therefore "builds theory." Both inductive and deductive approaches have been used in policy research in ESAMI MBA.

Another common classification of research divides research into applied and basic research. *Applied research* is research that is aimed at solving practical problems encountered in specific business environments. *Basic research* is conducted primarily to improve our understanding or knowledge of general issues. Basic research is also known as *pure, academic, fundamental, and theoretical* research. Table 1.3 shows a comparison between applied and basic research based on a number of criteria.

Table 1.3 Applied and Basic Research Compared

Applied Research	Basic Research
Purpose:	Purpose:
• Improve understanding of a particular business problem	• Expand knowledge of processes of business
• Results in a solution to the problem	• Results in universal principles relating to the process and its relationship to outcomes
• New knowledge limited to the problem	• Findings are of significance and value to society in general
• Findings are of particular relevance and value to managers in organizations	

Table 1.3 (Continued)

Context:	Context:
• Undertaken by people based in a variety of settings, including organizations and universities	• Undertaken by people based in universities
• Objectives negotiated with originator	• Choice of topic and objectives determined by the researcher
• Tight timescales	• Flexible timescales

Adopted from Saunders et al., 2007.

1.3 APPROACHES TO KNOWLEDGE GENERATION

The goal of a good research project is to create "true knowledge"; to others it means an "objective" investigation of empirical phenomena. Sekaran (2003) says that the conclusions drawn from the results of data analysis should be objective, that is, they should be based on the facts of the findings derived from actual values rather than our own subjective or emotional values. This means that even though you as a student may have started with personal experience and values, you should know that you need to obey the law of nature and keep your study free from personal biases.

Dunn (1981, p. 68) has come up with several approaches through which knowledge can be created. These were presented in a research methods textbook by Machmias (1981, p. 4). He argues that throughout history knowledge has been acquired by various *modes* or *approaches*. The major differences between these modes are the manner in which each places confidence in the producer of knowledge, the procedure by which knowledge is produced, and the effect of the knowledge produced.

These approaches are as follows.

1.   *The Authoritative Mode.* In the authoritative mode, knowledge is sought by referring to those socially superior or of an earlier

generation. The most common approach is to defer to those considered politically qualified, that is, "the authority". Different authorities seek to produce knowledge. The knowledge-seeker hence attributes the ability to produce knowledge to the social or political authority, e.g., "So-and-so said."

2. *The Mystical Mode.* In the mystical mode, knowledge is solicited from prophets, diviners, gods, or mediums. The mystical mode depends on:

   a. Manifestations of supernatural signs
   b. A psychological state to believe in the supernatural
   c. The rites surrounding the process of believing

   This mode applies ritualistic and ceremonial procedures done by the prophet or divine authority

3. *The Rationalistic Mode.* In the rationalistic mode, knowledge can be acquired by strict adherence to the forms and rules of logic. Underlying this approach are the assumptions that the human mind can comprehend the world and that what causes all events, and that which is logically possible and permissible has its form.

4. *The Scientific Approach.* The scientific approach is grounded on fundamental assumptions. These assumptions are considered to be necessary prerequisites for conducting of a *scientific* discourse.

In the MBA thesis we are expected to rely on the scientific mode of searching for knowledge.

1.4 THE SCIENTIFIC APPROACH

Some of the major claims in scientific research that need to be fulfilled include the following.

1. *There is an orderliness of events.* The scientific approach claims first that nature is orderly and regular, second that nature denotes all those empirically observable objects/conditions, and third that the law of nature does not prescribe but rather describes what actually is happening.

2. *Knowledge is superior to ignorance.* The scientific approach claims that relative knowledge is superior to and better than ignorance. The challenge in policy research is to find the knowledge, as ignorance has no defence.

3. *All natural phenomena have natural causes.* Science also claims that all natural phenomena have natural causes; therefore in life there are no accidents to events. There is always an X event triggering Y results. Hence nothing is self-evident, and anything that the student claims as truth must be demonstrated objectively in the thesis. It is not enough to say that the policy failed, for example, without showing the truth of the statement. In this approach possibilities for error are always present, because in many cases students confuse causes with effects and effects with causes.

4. *Knowledge is derived from the acquisition of experience.* Here its claims are based on the assumption that science must be empirical; it must rely on experience and observations. In this regard, the aim of the research report is to produce an accumulation of a body of reliable knowledge. Such knowledge will enable you to explain, predict, and understand an empirical phenomenon.

In the ESAMI thesis, therefore, your examiner will be asking or looking for a systematic and empirical analysis of the antecedent factors in the given situation that are responsible for the occurrence of the phenomenon.

Illustration 1: The student is interested in a company which she notes is having difficulties in financing operations because of the existing financial crisis. The research question could be, "What are the factors causing the failure to pay debts when they are due?"

The student, after literature review, could find many possible causes (X) causing the failure to pay debts (Y). The actual causes for failure to pay in this company will be found after field research.

Illustration 2: The student notes that there is a high attrition rate in the public service among graduates. This happens mainly after three years of service. The student is interested in finding out what caused this high attrition rate.

In both illustrations, the student must work at the scientific claims identified above to be able to get the proper explanation of the antecedents.

1.4.1   Deductive Explanation

The deductive approach uses a highly structured process. You need to start with a theory, law, or rule that becomes the basis for explanation. In deductive research you are testing a theory.

Robson (2002) presents useful steps to follow if one wants to use a deductive process. He presents simple guidelines as follows.

Step 1: You need to have a testable proposition about the relationship between specific events X and Y.

Examples:

1.   Students who attend classes do well in end-of-quarter examinations.
2.   An increase in incentives leads to an increase in productivity.

Step 2: You need to express this proposition in operational items. That is, you must indicate exactly how the concepts or variables are to be measured. You are proposing a relationship between specific concepts or variables.

Step 3: You need to test the operational hypothesis.

Step 4: You need to examine the specific outcome of the inquiry. This will either confirm or indicate the need for its modification.

Step 5: If necessary, you must modify the theory in the light of the findings. Saunders *et al.* (2007) says that in deductive thinking you search to explain the causal relationship between variables. Here you should always remember first that an important characteristic of deductive reasoning is to have controls to allow testing of the hypothesis and second that those controls ensure that the changes in Y are a function of X and no other factors.

Quiz:

When I see Mary, I see Joan.
Joan is around.
Mary is around.

Is this a true or false statement?

Quiz:

When I see Mary, John is around.
Mary is around.
Therefore, John is around.
Is this a true or false statement?

1.4.2 Induction or Probabilistic Explanation

In research, not all explanations are based on laws of universal form. Sometimes you will find that there is only a high probability that an event will bring the occurrence.

We saw earlier that induction is a process where we observe certain phenomenon, and on this basis we arrive at a conclusion (Sekaran, 2003, p. 23).

In inductive reasoning you build theory from observation. You should first take into account an understanding of the way in which humans interpret their social world. In this approach research focuses on the context in which events are taking place and thus requires a sample followed by research. You collect data, and then you build theory from the data. The purpose here is for you to get a feel of what is going on. First define the research problem. Then the task is to make sense of the collected data. The result of that analysis will be the formulation of a theory.

Many students have said that inductive research methodology is more flexible than deductive research.

The following example illustrates a typical inductive process.

1. You make an empirical observation by reading from factory records. You find that productivity levels were higher when the weather was cooler.
2. You come to a conclusion that employees work harder in cold weather.
3. You come up with the theory that cooler weather leads to high productivity.

In the theses done at ESAMI, both deduction and induction have been used by students to understand, explain, or predict outcomes.

Example:

In our intakes, many of the students like testing the Maslow hierarchy of needs theory in the African setting. Quite a number of the students begin with this theory. For example, the most common statement is:

"Self-actualization increases performance."

Then a hypothesis is generated.

"If an employee is involved in decision making, his/her productivity increases."

Based on the above logic, the student conducts the research to confirm or disconfirm the hypothesis.

In the above illustration the student started with a theory—Maslow's Hierarchy of Needs—and then built a hypothesis and logically deducted from the results of the field study.

1.4.3   Prediction

In research, we have noted that prediction constitutes another component of scientific knowledge generation. This is because the ability to predict correctly is the first quality for identifying what is science. It can also be taken to be a key success criterion for any manager. Everybody wishes they could predict correctly what will happen to their company's performance ten years from today. However, prediction is the reverse of the process of explanation.

Example:

Antecedents record facts that initial conditions are present. We also know that universal laws or probabilistic generalizations can be used to justify the prediction that if initial conditions are present then the consequence must follow.

Hence, for example, if you know the relationship between X and Y—that is $Y = f(X_1 + X_2 + X_3)$—then you can also predict what will happen to Y if any of Xs changed.

By knowing X_1, X_2, and X_3, we are able to predict the future.

1.4.4   Causal Inferences

At the heart of scientific explanations is the idea of causality, that is, what the independent variable is expected to produce in the dependent variable in the direction and magnitude specified by the theory. In research, managers are looking for data. For example, if we note that the increase in the use of e-commerce reduces the cost of doing business, then e-commerce is the *independent* variable "producing' the reduction in the cost of doing business (the *dependent* variable). Or in the example we saw earlier, the relationship between job satisfaction and job performance. Job satisfaction is the independent variable and job performance the dependent variable.

Hence the time order demonstrates that one phenomenon occurs first or changes prior to another phenomenon. That is, the change in e-commerce occurs first, and then we see the reduction in the cost of doing business. In some studies, students investigate *causality*; in others they study *covariation*, which is expressed through measures of relations commonly referred to as correlations or associations. Covariation means that two or more factors vary together. For example, a student found out that a change in education levels was accompanied by a change in income, personal savings, and democratic values.

The two major approaches are shown in Figure 1.1. The left arm shows the inductive approach, the right arm the deductive.

Figure 1.1 Summary of key approaches—inductive and deductive process. Adapted from Sekaran (2003, p. 28).

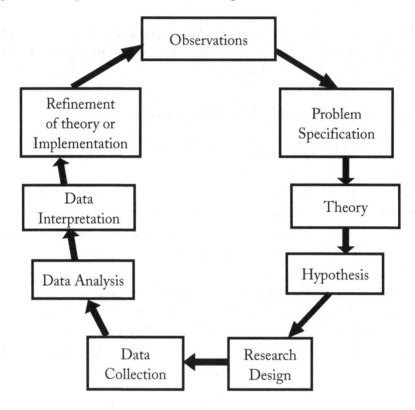

1.5 RESEARCH PROBLEMS

A problem is an intellectual stimulus calling for an answer in the form of scientific inquiry. Managers face many policy problems requiring solutions. The challenge in decision-making is whether one is solving the right problem or not.

A *research problem* can be defined as any situation where a gap exists between the actual and the desired ideal states (Sekaran, 2003, p. 29). A problem for research can also be a mere issue that requires some right answers for a situation to be improved. Problems must be clearly and specifically articulated for them to be empirically solved by research.

Problems must be distinguished from mere symptoms. In the example of job satisfaction influencing job performance, it may be that low job satisfaction is just a symptom of deep-rooted morale and motivation problems. Identifying the real problem is the key in finding the right solution to the problem.

1.6 UNIT OF ANALYSIS

The identification of a research problem requires the identification of the *unit of analysis* for the study. The unit of analysis refers to the level of aggregation of the data to be collected in order to come up with a solution to the problem. The researcher must specify whether the level of aggregation will focus on the entire economy, sectors, organizations, departments, work groups, individuals, or objects. The decision on the unit of analysis will affect data collection methods, sample size, and even the variables in the conceptual or theoretical framework.

Examples:

1. If the statement focuses on individual levels of employees in general, then we are interested in *individuals*.
2. If we are interested in two-people interaction, then several two-person groups known as *dyads* become the unit of analysis, e.g., husband and wife, supervisor and subordinate.
3. If we are studying group effectiveness, then the unit of analysis is the *group*.
4. If we are studying the effectiveness of reforms in Africa, then the unit of analysis becomes *nations*.

CHAPTER TWO

ORGANISING YOUR MBA POLICY THESIS

Your MBA policy thesis must be organized in a logical and scientific manner.

2.1 RESEARCH PROBLEM AREA

How do you choose a research problem?

Interest. What is your interest? What are you passionate about? For example, is your passion one of the following topics we saw among the completed theses?

- fighting poverty
- fighting corruption
- fighting HIV/AIDS
- customer Care
- globalization
- sustainability

Problems. Policy theses are about solving problems in order to obtain a solution. Look for problems requiring solutions. For example, here are some typical problems.

1. Sales volume has been going down in the past three years at XYZ Ltd.
2. In your organization, staff turnover has been rising in the past two years.
3. XYX Ltd. is losing market share in your country.
4. Customer complaints have been rising at XYZ Ltd.

Observation. Observe what is going on in your organization's environment and focus on the problems or issues that need to be addressed for your organization to move forward in this changing environment.

Strengths. What are your strengths? Your strengths may lie in your academic background or in your career experience. For example, if you have accounting qualifications, it should be relatively easy for you to identify accounting-related research problems and issues. Or, if you have accounting qualifications but somehow you have spent the past ten years in human resource management, it should be relatively easy to identify human resource management research problems and issues.

2.2   CHALLENGES IN SELECTION OF THE RESEARCH PROBLEM

Defining a policy research problem involves several interrelated steps, which can set out as follows (Zikmund, 2003, p. 94).

1. Identify the problem through observation and focusing.
2. Understand the background of the problem through a situation analysis.
3. Isolate and identify the problem rather than its symptoms.
4. Determine the unit of analysis in this problem "mess".
5. Determine the relevant variables and how they relate to each other.
6. State the research questions (hypotheses) and research objectives.

A policy research problem must be an important one. An important problem is one that has the following qualities (Mugenda and Mugenda, 1999).

1. It leads to findings that have widespread implications in a particular area.
2. It must challenge some commonly held truism.
3. It should review the inadequacies of existing law, views, and policies.
4. It should cover sufficient scope that you will fulfil the school page requirements for the MBA thesis by writing it.

2.3   *LITERATURE REVIEW*

The purposes of literature review in a policy research are many. We think the following should guide you to choose which literature is useful in your study.

1. We review existing literature in order to show what studies have been done so far which are relevant to your own research. Literature review must help you to find out what others have already researched, learned, and reported on your topic so that you may take account of this in the design of your study. This helps you avoid re-inventing the wheel.
2. Through literature review, you obtain ideas of how to handle your research problem. It helps you to further understand the problem you plan to research on, and this may lead you to refine the statement of the problem.
3. Literature review provides you some sources of information, facts, data, methods, and techniques of research you did not know about. It gives you familiarity with the various types of methodologies that others have used that may give you a guideline of how you may develop your own method or methodology of dealing with the same policy problem.

4. Literature review introduces you to authors of books or research and reports that you had not previously read.

5. Literature review helps you generate a number of alternative subjects and key words that others never used before or have misapplied to Africa.

6. Literature review helps you decide which subjects to pursue. It helps you to see your research study in perspective and in relation to past research dealing with similar problems, but in an African context

7. Literature review helps you make a decision on which subjects or problems to abandon.

8. Literature review is part of the process of topic selection. That is, after reading broadly, you may then select a topic you would want to pursue with regard to your broad "issues" in your organization.

Literature review should focus around the problem area or gaps in previous research. A good literature review should be critical, comprehensive, and contextual. It should provide the reader with a theory base and a survey of published works that relate to the problem being researched.

In the literature review, you should read published works by researchers and other management thinkers in the research problem area in order to identify areas that were overlooked by researchers in the past. These gaps should be the focus of your current study if you are to make a difference.

Major theories, models, and management thinking advanced by past thinkers and researchers should be analysed and should provide a linkage to your current problem. Where research questions have been developed, these can be used as subsections in the literature review. Under these subsections, write about gaps in past research that attempted to investigate similar research questions. You make a case for your study by arguing your case to focus on these gaps.

The literature review is not where you give a chronology of books read in the past. It must be a critical review of knowledge as it relates to your topic.

2.4 *PROBLEM STATEMENT*

Let us go back to what we said is an important stage in the statement of the policy research problem. If you have identified a general/broad area of study, it should be narrowed down using information gathered through talking to experts in the area and a review of the literature. Narrowing down the problem should lead to a *problem statement.*

The problem statement is a clear and precise statement of the question or issue that is to be investigated with the zeal of finding an answer or solution to the issue or problem. The purpose of the policy research must be stated as part of the problem statement, indicating also the target population of your study.

Here are some characteristics of a good problem statement (Mugenda and Mugenda, 1999, p. 19).

1. It should be written clearly, capturing the reader's interest.
2. The specific problem should be objectively researchable.
3. The scope should be clearly indicated.
4. The importance of the study in adding new knowledge should be stated.
5. The purpose of the research should be stated.

You can start a problem statement with a *general focus research question* which flows directly from your research idea or problem area. This may lead to several more detailed *research questions* or the definition of *research objectives.* Table 2.1 shows an example of a research idea and a corresponding general focus research question.

Table 2.1 Research Idea and General Focus Research Question

Research Idea	General Focus Research Question
The future of trade unions in Southern Africa	What are the strategies that trade unions in Southern Africa should adopt to ensure their future viability?
The sponsorship of football clubs in East Africa	What benefit do multinational companies get from sponsoring football clubs in East Africa?
Downsizing and the long-range growth patterns of companies in Kenya	What are the effects of downsizing on the long-range growth patterns of companies in Kenya?

Here we move from the general idea of "the future of trade unions in Southern Africa" (as opposed to Europe or Asia). The research question is narrowed to "strategies to survive" as opposed to "strategies to close".

Policy research questions and policy research objectives should also be derived directly from the *purpose statement*. Table 2.2 shows an example of this relationship.

Table 2.2 Example of Elements of a Problem Statement

General Focus Research Question:	What is the relationship between resource management skills and performance in small-scale businesses owned by women in rural areas of Malawi?

Table 2.2 (Continued)

Purpose:	The purpose of this study is to explore the influence of resource management skills on the performance of small-scale businesses owned by women in rural areas of Malawi.	
Research Objectives	**Research Questions**	**Research Hypotheses or Proposition**
To identify the socio-economic status of small-scale business women in rural areas of Malawi.	What is the socio-economic status of small-scale business women in rural areas of Malawi?	The socio-economic status of small-scale business women in rural Malawi has risen by at least 10% since 1985.
To investigate the saving practices of women in rural areas of Malawi.	What are the saving practices of women in rural Malawi?	Rural women in Malawi do not bank their money with large commercial banks.
To investigate the financial management practices of women in rural areas of Malawi.	What are the financial management practices of women in rural Malawi?	Wrong financial management practices lead to bankruptcy in businesses owned by women in rural Malawi.
To determine the level of knowledge of management processes among women in rural areas of Malawi.	What is the level of knowledge amongst women in rural areas of Malawi?	Poor knowledge of management processes lead to poor performance of businesses owned by women in rural Malawi.

One general area may lead to many different research activities. It is very important at this stage to have a proper logical framework that links your policy research idea or problem to research purposes and objectives to hypothesis or proportions. You should be satisfied that this relation is both logical and researchable. Remember that what you put in this part of the research is the social contract you have with your examiner. In the end, the examiner will want to see how your research problem, purpose, objectives, and hypothesis were handled in your research.

2.5 *DEVELOPING THE THEORETICAL FRAMEWORK*

Given the School's requirement that your study must have a methodology, you might ask where this methodology comes from. After conducting the literature review and defining the research problem, you should be ready to develop the theoretical framework. The *theoretical framework* is the conceptual model of how one theorizes or makes logical sense of the relationships among the factors or *variables* that have been identified as important to the problem (Sekaran, 2003, p. 87). The *theory* should flow logically from the literature review and from your own beliefs about the problem situation. The theory is a coherent set of general *propositions* used as principles to explain the apparent relationships of certain observed phenomena. The theoretical framework provides the scientific basis for investigating the research problem. From the theoretical framework, propositions and hypotheses are deduced; hence they can be tested. This enhances our understanding of the problem situation dynamics. Behavioural predictions of the factors can also be easily made.

2.5.1 Definitions of Key Terms

Methodology has four related elements, namely:

1. *Theory.* A coherent set of general propositions used to explain the apparent relationships among certain observed phenomena. In the "Women in Rural Malawi" example, it is presumed that management skills make a difference in one's progress in a small-scale business.
2. *Variable.* Any characteristic that assumes different numerical values. There are many management skills one might identify, but in this example "saving practices" are identified as making a difference in the performance of small-scale businesses.

3. *Proposition.* A statement concerned with the relationships among variables. The proposition here is that knowledge, saving practices, and performance are related.

4. *Hypothesis.* An empirically testable proposition. Here the hypothesis is that those who have knowledge about saving practices do well in their business and the alternative is that those who don't, fail.

2.5.2   Variables

The first step in developing the theoretical framework is to identify the factors (variables) that help characterize the problem situation and dynamics. These are variables from which propositions and hypotheses can easily be made.

There are four main types of variables our students have encountered. These are:

- the dependent variable
- the independent variable
- the moderating variable
- the intervening variable

2.5.3   The Dependent Variable

This is the variable of primary importance to the researcher. The researcher's aim is to explain this variable, to measure it under various conditions, and to predict its future state.

Examples:

1. The influence of poverty on the nutritional status of African children. The dependent variable is "nutritional status of African children".

2. The impact of downsizing on corporate performance at XYZ Ltd. The dependent variable is "corporate performance".

2.5.4   The Independent Variable

This is the variable that works to influence the dependent variable. In the example above, "poverty" and "downsizing" are the independent variables in the two examples, respectively.

In most policy researches, independent variables are called X and dependent variables are called Y. Depending on the research, X can be many variables contributing to the change in Y.

Example:

$$Y = f(X_1, X_2, X_3, \ldots X_n)$$

In our Malawi example:

Y = Level of performance
X_1 = Level of education
X_2 = Saving practices
X_3 = Number of dependents

2.5.5   The Moderating Variable

This is the variable that has a strong contingent effect on the relationship between the independent and the dependent variables. It moderates and helps explain this relationship.

Example:

Studying the influence of poverty on the nutritional status of African children, one may find that "government macro-economic policies" are a possible moderating variable.

2.5.6   The Intervening Variable

This is the variable that surfaces between the time the independent variable starts to operate on the dependent variable and the time the impact is manifested in the dependent variable. It surfaces as a function of the independent variable, and helps explain the influence of the independent variable on the dependent variable.

Example:

Take a proposition that staff on-the-job retooling influences corporate performance. However, you notice from the literature that corporate performance cannot be influenced directly. Staff on-the-job retooling must result in job satisfaction and motivation first. Hence "job satisfaction" and "motivation" are intervening variables. Due to time constraints in most MBA research studies, there will be very little time to measure intervening variables as they tend to be longitudinal in nature.

2.5.7   Other "Extraneous" Variables

Extraneous variables are variables of which you are not aware that may influence your research results. The nature of the influence may be positive or negative. Extraneous variables can be any of the three variables described above—intervening, moderating, or independent variables. If extraneous variables are known in advance, then you need to control them in your research. In this case, extraneous variables become *control variables*. The most common and rational way of identifying extraneous variables is through the literature review, especially of past research. A control variable can be a *covariate variable*, a *concomitant variable*, or a *blocking variable*. Building control variables into your research significantly enhances the *validity* of your research results.

The following methods are commonly used to control for extraneous variables.

1. You can build the variables into your research design.
2. You can hold the variables constant, that is, consider only one level or category of the variable during measurement.
3. You can smooth the effects of an extraneous variable using statistical techniques such as covariance analysis and partial correlation analysis.

The common types of extraneous variables include the following:

1. *Antecedent variable.* This is a variable which precedes an independent variable.
2. *Intervening variable.* This is a variable which appears between the time an independent variable starts to operate on the dependent variable and the time the impact is manifested in the dependent variable. It appears as a function of the independent variable.
3. *Suppressor variable.* This is a variable which makes a true relationship disappear.
4. *Distorter variable.* This is a variable which changes the sign of a given relation, say from positive to negative or vice versa.

2.6 MEASUREMENT AND OPERATIONAL DEFINITION

After coming this far, the next important step in preparing for your policy research is to address the issues of measurement and operational definition of your key variables. We are calling it "locating meaning to your variables". Avoid the use of vague language.

The issue is to what extent your meaning reflects the reality, and most importantly, how that meaning will help you collect and analyse your data. To come up with smart measurement and operational definition, the following can help you.

1. First, you need to consider all variables in your theoretical framework and how they will be operationalized and measured.
2. Second, you should look at behaviour, facets, or properties denoted by the concept, and then you translate these into observable elements.
3. Third, you should develop a questionnaire to measure the elements identified.

2.6.1 The Congruence Problem

There several issues in research that arise in moving from a concept to empirical observation. The degree of *congruence* between conceptual definition and operational definition must be handled carefully. For example, intelligence is defined conceptually as the ability to think abstractly, and to measure intelligence, we use an intelligence test in the operational definition of the ability to think abstractly.

When you are moving from a concept to an operational definition, the question is what is the degree of congruence between the two definitions that is conceptual and operational?

2.6.2 Illustration of Movement from Concept to Operational Definition

The theory level will provide:

- a conceptual level of understanding of the phenomena
- a conceptual definition, which is your definition of those key concepts

You then need to move from theory to research level. Here you need to come up with the operational definitions. These definitions will then be used at the observational level.

Examples:

1. What is operational definition of poverty?
2. What behavioural dimension, facets, or characteristics would we find called "poverty"?

Figure 2.1 Behavioural Dimensions of the Concept "Poverty"

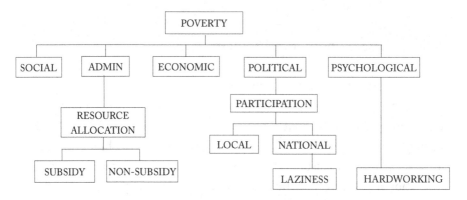

If poverty is conceptualised as powerlessness, how can we determine it? What set of questions are we going to ask to measure powerlessness?

To understand poverty, we may have to build a set of questions for each dimension whose answers will help us measure the level of poverty. The issue of validity is concerned with the question of whether you are measuring what you think should be measured. Nachmias and Nachmias (1976, p. 59) identify three basic kinds of validity. Each type of validity is be used for different types of measurement.

1. *Content Validity*. Two types of content validity are identified, namely *face validity* and *sampling validity*. Sampling is covered in Chapter 5. Face validity concerns the extent to which the instrument being used measures that which it appears to measure according to your subjective assessment (Nachmias and Nachmias, 1976). Sampling validity concerns the representativeness of the sample with respect to the population

from which it is drawn, and how large the sample is in order to make valid conclusions about the population under study.

2. *Empirical Validity.* There should be a relationship between the measuring instrument you are using and the measurement results. Predictive validity will be used to evaluate empirical validity.

3. *Construct Validity.* To have construct validity, you must relate your measuring instrument to an overall theoretical framework in order to determine whether the instrument you are using is tied to the assumptions and concepts you are using (Campbell and Fiske, 1959).

2.7 *DEVELOPMENT OF HYPOTHESES*

Some of our students like working with hypotheses. Remember, not all studies will start with one hypothesis.

In a quantitative research, we work with hypotheses to be confirmed or rejected. The hypotheses will be built between X and Y and built from the subsets of the theoretical framework.

2.7.1 Schematic Relationship

Several steps need to be followed to come up with a good hypothesis. First, remember that the theoretical framework gives us a relationship between key variables. For example, if our interest is in studying why there has been an increase in road safety violations in Kenya. You might hypothesise the reasons to be one of the following:

- training of drivers
- drivers communicating with cell phones while driving
- narrow roads
- driving defective vehicles
- too many cars on the road

In this case, in the theoretical framework you need to rearrange these variables into logical relationships. Some of these variables could be moderating variables, intervening variables, antecedents etc. It is important to remember that here you need to hypothesise that safety violations are caused by something, say "drivers communicating with cell phone while driving", while "training of drivers" is a moderating variable.

2.7.2   Hypotheses Development

Once you have developed the theoretical framework and come up with the relation between those variables, then are able to:

1.   Test these relationships through appropriate statistical analyses or through negative case analysis in qualitative research.
2.   Change the situation in order to solve the problem.

2.7.3   Definitions of "Hypothesis"

There are many definitions of "hypothesis" in the textbooks on research methods, but here we are looking at a process of formulating testable statements or propositions. Hence, a logically conjectured relationship between two or more variables expressed in the form of a testable statement is a hypothesis.

In the example of road safety issues, you might hypothesise that if drivers are given adequate training, safety violations will be reduced. Then you can go out and collect data on the extent of training given to various drivers and the number of safety violations committed. You can statistically examine the relationship between these two variables. Is there a difference between the number of accidents committed by drivers who have gone through a comprehensive training on road use and safety and those who haven't?

If you find the case to be true, then the hypothesis is accepted, or it can be rejected if no significant relationship exists between training and safety violations. This assumes other factors have been controlled.

2.7.4   Formats of Statements of Hypotheses

There are many formats to present hypothesis statements. Common formats are described below.

If-Then Statements

Examples:

1.   When employees are satisfied, they will perform better.
2.   If employees are more satisfied with the job, then they will absent themselves less frequently.

In these two illustrations we have two different types of hypothesis statements. That is, satisfaction then performance, and satisfaction then no absenteeism.

Directional Hypotheses

If in stating a relationship between variables you use terms such as positive/negative/more than/less than and the like, then these hypotheses are called directional. The direction of the relationship between variables (positive or negative) is indicated.

Examples:

1.   Competition is tougher in the Kenyan market than in Tanzania.
2.   Younger employees work harder than older employees.
3.   There is negative correlation between the age of employees and job satisfaction.

The direction of the relationship is indicated in the hypothesis.

Non-Directional Hypotheses

Sometimes you will work with hypotheses that do postulate a relationship or a difference but offer no indication of the direction of this relationship or difference. That is, there is a relationship, but you may not be able to conjecture whether the relationship is negative or positive.

The following statements illustrate these relationships:

1. There is a relationship between age and job satisfaction.
2. There is a difference between the work ethical values of male and female employees.

In both cases you are not sure which way the relationship will go.

These types of hypotheses are formulated because the relationship or differences have never been previously explored. Hence, you have no basis for indicating the direction. They may also be formulated when there have been conflicting findings in previous research on the variables and their relationship.

We have various conflicting discussions, but no comprehensive research seems to have been done in Africa. To test these interesting relationships, one is interested in finding out whether in Africa, age and corruption or gender and corruption are related.

The Null and the Alternate Hypotheses

Most researchers work with two types of hypotheses called the *Null* and the *Alternate* (or *Alternative*) hypotheses.

A Null hypothesis is a proposition that states a definitive exact relationship between variables that is equal to zero or that the difference in the means of two groups in the population is equal to zero (or some definite number).

For example, a Null hypothesis can be stated that there is no (significant) relationship between two variables, for example, that there is no significant relationship between gender and the incidence of corruption in the workplace.

In this Null hypothesis, we expect to see that

$$H_o: M_M = M_W$$
Or
$$H_o: M_M - M_W = 0$$

Where H_o is the Null hypothesis, M_W is the mean incidence of corruption among women, and M_M is the mean incidence of corruption among men.

The Alternate hypothesis is the opposite hypothesis to the Null hypothesis. This hypothesis can be directional.

The Alternate directional hypothesis will be stated like this:

$$H_A: M_M < M_w$$

Which is the same as

$$H_A: M_W > M_M$$

Where H_A represents the Alternate hypothesis, and M_W and M_M are the mean incidences of corruption among women and men respectively.

2.7.5 Choosing A Statistical Test

Having formulated the Null and Alternate hypotheses, you should remember that an appropriate statistical test (t-test, F-test, etc.) needs to be applied to indicate whether or not support has been found for the Alternate. That is, there is a significant relationship between groups or there is a significant relationship between variables as hypothesised. In other words, age and corruption are related or gender and corruption are related.

CHAPTER THREE

RESEARCH DESIGN

After developing the theoretical framework and relevant hypotheses, you need to design the study. The aim of a research design is that it should guide the process of data collection and the analysing and interpreting of what you will observe. Two major concerns in designing a study are internal and external validity issues.

3.1   BASIC ELEMENTS IN A GOOD DESIGN

Let us look at some of the things you need to remember in order to be able to come up with a good research design.

1. You need to know and identify the type of study you are conducting.
2. You must identify the required statistical tests appropriate for your study.
3. Your study may be either exploratory, descriptive, hypothesis testing, or case-study analysis.

Remember that we said earlier that the nature of the study would depend on the stage to which knowledge about your research topic has advanced. However, research design becomes rigorous as you move from the exploratory stage, where you attempt to explore new ideas for research, to the descriptive stage, where you try to describe certain characteristics of a phenomenon, to hypothesis testing, where you examine whether or not the conjectured relationship has been supported and if the answer to the research question has been obtained.

3.1.1 Types of Study

There are four types of study:

1. *Exploratory Studies.* This type of study is undertaken when not so much is known about the situation; no information is available on how similar problems or research issues have been solved in the past. Please remember that doing a research study for first time in an organization does not make it exploratory. It is only exploratory when knowledge is scarce and a deeper understanding is sought. In this case, interviewing has been found to be the best technique. You interview individuals or focus groups to explore the issues.

2. *Descriptive Studies.* This type of study is undertaken when you want to ascertain and be able to describe the characteristics of interest. The goal in a descriptive study is to provide a profile of an aspect of interest.

3. *Hypothesis Testing.* This type of study is appropriate when your aim is to explain the nature of a relationship or to establish the difference among groups or the independence of variables.

4. *Case-Study Analysis.* Most of our students do case studies. But you need to know how far a case study can go. Usually, case-study analysis is undertaken when you aim at conducting an in-depth contextual analysis of matters relating to a similar situation.

3.1.2 Types of Investigation

Since there are different types of studies, you need to decide on the following issues before you design your study. You should establish whether a *causal* or *correlation* study is needed to answer the research question. In a *causal study*, it is necessary to establish a definitive cause-and-effect relationship or else you will be dealing with a *correlation study*. If you want a mere identification of the important factors associated with the problem, you identify factors associated with it rather than establishing a cause-and-effect relationship.

The difference between the two can be illustrated using the common example of the relationship between smoking and cancer.

In a causal study, the research question is easily illustrated. Does smoking cause cancer?

In a correlation study, the research questions might be:

1. Are smoking and cancer related?
2. Are smoking, drinking, and chewing tobacco associated with cancer? If so, which of these contributes most to the variance in the dependent variable?

Cancer = f (smoking, drinking beer, chewing tobacco, etc.)

The questions are all about cancer and smoking, but the answer to the first question will help establish whether or not people who do not smoke will not develop cancer. The answer to the second question will determine whether smoking and cancer are correlated. In asking the third question, you recognize that there are perhaps several other factors that influence cancer apart from smoking—maybe beer, maybe tobacco.

But do these three variables explain a significant amount of the variance in cancer? If they do, which of them has greatest association with it?

The answer to a correlation study will help determine the extent of risk of cancer that people expose themselves by smoking, drinking, and chewing tobacco.

You can move from this commonly used smoking/cancer topic to the more recent discussion on what makes a country globally competitive.

Casual Study: Good governance causes a country to be globally competitive.

Correlation Study: Countries with effective systems of governance tend to be globally competitive.

In this regard the intention is not to establish cause and effect but to see if a relationship does exist among the variables investigated.

You can see that the type of study will definitely influence how you will organize your study and what you will be working on. Two of us can be working on the issue of tobacco and cancer, but we end up designing different studies—that is, causal versus correctional studies.

3.3.3   Study Setting

When designing your study, you also need to decide on the nature of your study setting. A study setting can be contrived (a laboratory) or non-contrived (an organization). Studies done in non-contrived settings are also known as field studies. You can design a correlation study to be done in a non-contrived (organization) setting or a rigorous causal study to be done in contrived lab setting when you want to establish a cause-effect relationship.

As an example of a field study, one of our recent students carried out a study involving an analysis of the relationship between interest rates and various bank deposit patterns of clients. She took balances in various types of accounts and correlated them to changes in interest rates. In order to do this field experiment, she selected four branches of the banks that charged differing interest rates. Her aim was to determine if there is an effect on deposit mobilization in the branches. Differing interest rates were taken to be equivalent to manipulating interest rates.

Her findings showed that there is no relationship between interest rates and bank deposit patterns.

3.2 RESEARCH DESIGN TYPES

There are several types of research designs ranging from pre-experiment to experiments. We review each one of these below.

From our observation, experimental designs are not feasible for most of our MBA thesis projects. Saunders *et al.* (2007, p. 137) sums up the steps in an experiment:

- definition of a theoretical hypothesis
- selection of samples from known positions
- random allocation of samples to different experimental conditions; the experimental and control subjects
- introduction of planned interventions or manipulation to one or more of the variables
- control of all other variables

3.2.1   Pre-Experimental Designs

Issues to consider if you want to use a pre-experimental design are:

1. When the phenomena is not amenable to straight forward application of experimental designs
2. When the ethical/political/social reasons may impede controlled experts.
3. Time interval demands, e.g. time between stimulus and response *vis-a-vis* property disposition.
4. Sometimes degree of specificity in respect of the stimulus has a direct bearing on how easy or difficult it will be to isolate the desired property e.g. employment *vis-a-vis* social class

The weaknesses of these study designs are many. They pertain to the general weakness of all pre-experimental designs; for instance, an individual in the group might have started differently initially with respect to dependent variable measured. It means that the groups were not equivalent before introducing of X (see discussion between pre-test and post-test experimental design).

In the remainder of this section, we will examine examples of pre-experimental designs.

Design 1: One-Shot Case Study

This is a common pre-experimental design used by some of the students in research. It is also called pre-test and post-test group design. It involves the observation of a single group or event or firm's policy at a single time subsequent to a phenomenon or treatment. After the introduction of the treatment (X), then one observes O_2 after. That is why this design is called "before and after without control design" and is characterized as:

$$O_1 \, X \, O_2$$

O_1 represents the phenomenon before treatment X is introduced. O_2 is the phenomenon after the treatment. The impact of the treatment is the difference $O_2 - O_1$.

Illustration 1. A student studied the introduction of universal free primary education (X) and its impact on numbers five years later. The effect of the treatment is the difference between O_2 and O_1. The design looks like: $O_1 \, X \, O_2$.

O_1 is the number at primary level before the policy; and the policy X is universal free primary education; O_2 is the number after the policy.

<u>Illustration 2.</u> A student studied the impact of e-election (X) on the number of people who voted (O_2). O_1 is the number who voted before e-election; X is the introduction of e-election; O_2 is the number of voters after e-election technology was introduced

Design 2: After-Only with Control

This is also called "Post-test only with experimental and control groups". In this design the dependent variable Y is measured in both the treatment and control groups. The impact of the treatment (X) is assessed by subtracting the value of the dependent variable in the control from its value in the treatment group (O_1 - O_2).

Experimental Group: X 0_1
Control Group: 0_2

Design 3: Before and After with Control

Experimental Group: O_1 X O_2
Control Group: O_3 O_4

Here two areas are selected, and the dependent variable is measured in both groups for a period before the treatment. Treatment is introduced within one group only. Then the dependent variables are measured in both groups from an identified period after introduction of the treatment.

The effect is determined by subtracting the change in the dependent variable in the experimental group from the change in the control group, that is, O_2 - O_4.

These commonly used pre-experimental designs are the weakest of all research designs. Really, they can't measure the true cause-and-effect relationship. That is why they are always referred to as quasi-experimental designs. In the pre-test and post-test design, the testing and instrumentation effects contaminate the internal validity. Sekaran also adds that "if the experiment is extended over a period of time, *history* and *maturation* effects may also confound the results" (Sekaran, 2003, p. 150).

Even in cases where students have introduced control groups, since the groups were not matched, possible contamination from nuisance variables such as selection bias and mortality can still confound the results.

Design 4: Time Series

In this design, students compare data from various years in the past before the policy or program under study was introduced. This is called a time-series design. In this study design, the student uses historical data to analyse observations on the variable of interest. At least three sets of measures before and after introduction of the independent variable are used. For example, a student in 2010 wanted to study the impact of affirmative action introduced in 1980. She organized a time-series data around the point when the policy was introduced. She observed before and after the changes in the variable of interest, the number of women in parliament.

A time-series design looks like this:

$$O_1 O_2 O_3 X O_4 O_5 O_6$$

The Os are the observations on the variable of interest (women in parliament) at different historical times. The X variable is the policy (affirmative action) introduced in 1980.

When using this design, care must be taken. As Julian L. Simon says, the "essential ingredient to obtaining valid results with the design is that the independent variable(s) in which you are interested must have varied due to reasons unrelated to the nature of the sample period or sample individuals" (Simon, 1978, p. 174). The only strength is that the several observations make it possible to separate the reactive measurement effects. Students must therefore take care when using time-series designs, as the longer the time period, the higher the chances that changes could come from maturation or passage of time. That is, shifts occur when values of the variable of interest (the number of women) are selected upon the basis of extreme scores.

Design 5: Least Elaborated Comparison Group

In this design, members are assigned as members of a group or category based on a shared attribute. Members of each group are then measured with respect to the dependent variable between periods. For example, a student studied the performance of different banks situated in different cities or provinces of the country to study whether size and location affected the performance of the branches. Here we are examining the effect of more than one variable (size and location) as the independent variable and performance as the dependent variable.

Bank Size

Large   Small

	Large	Small
Rural	1	2
Urban	3	4

Location

The four experimental groups have four different "treatments" representing all possible combinations of values of the two variables.

1. Large Size—Rural Location
2. Small Size—Rural Location
3. Large Size—Urban Location
4. Small Size—Urban Location

Hence there are four treatments:

$$R\,X_1\,O_1$$
$$R\,X_2\,O_2$$
$$R\,X_3\,O_3$$
$$R\,X_4\,O_4$$

Design 6: Factorial

Factorial designs are supposed to increase the external validity of the study. When two or more manipulations are done in an independent variable, the other designs discussed early are not very useful. Therefore, the factorial design does help to study two or more treatments and their joint effects can be assessed.

General Remarks on Pre-Experimental Design

The internal validity of pre-experimental designs is weak. Too many intrinsic and extrinsic variables are not controlled. Hence, any inferences drawn are inconclusive.

These designs are useful for exploratory researches. They can lead to exploratory researches that may lead to an insight that could be studied. These designs can't be used for hypothesis testing.

3.2.2   Classic Experimental Design

To use these designs you will need to organize your study in a more rigorous manner than in most pre-experimented designs. The basic elements of a classical experimental design centre on the following:

	Pre-Test		Post-Test	Difference
Experimental Group	$R\,O_1$	X	O_2	$O_2 - O_1 - d_e$
Control Group	$R\,O_3$		O_4	$O_4 - O_3 = d_c$

X is the independent variable; the Os are measurements on the dependent variable; R is the random assignment of subjects to experiment and control group; and d_e and d_c are the difference between the post-test and pre-test in each group (Nachmias and Nachmias, 1976, p. 30; Sekaran, 2003, p. 160).

The subjects in the experimental group are tested before and after being exposed to the treatment. The control group is tested twice, at the same times as the experimental group.

The treatment effect will be calculated as follows:

$$(O_2 - O_1) - (O_4 - O_3).$$

Example:

There is awareness of a new government agricultural subsidy policy among 20 per cent of the subjects ($O_1 = 20\%$, $O_3 = 20\%$) before a sensitization campaign. After exposure to the treatment, there is a 35 per cent awareness in the experimental group ($O_2 = 35\%$) and a 22 per cent awareness in the control group ($O_4 = 22\%$). The treatment effect equals 13 per cent:

$$(0.35 - 0.20) - (0.22 - 0.20) = (0.15 - 0.02) = 0.13 \text{ or } 13\%$$

To assess the effect of the independent variable, you measure the dependent variable in the experimental group as follows:

Before treatment—the pre-test
After treatment—the post-test

This process helps you to deal with the reactive effect of testing which can be directly measured by comparing the experimental groups and control groups. The comparison will indicate whether X has an independent effect on the groups.

The classical design has been modified but has not lost the basic requirement to increase internal and external validity. Here we describe two modifications of the classical experiment design.

Modification 1: Post-Test Only Control Group

$$R \: X \: O_1$$
$$R \: O_2$$

Here you omit the pre-tested groups altogether. This design can control all intrinsic sources of invalidity. Randomisation is done to both groups—experimental and control.

Modification 2: The Solomon Four-Group

Pre-Test		Post-Test
R	O_1 X	O_2
R	O_3	O_4
R	X	O_5
R		O_6

This design is the same as the classical design, but additional sets of control and experimental groups are added that are not pre-tested.

The effects are then compared as follows:

$$O_2 > O_1$$
$$O_2 > O_4$$
$$O_5 > O_6$$
$$O_5 > O_3$$

If these are in agreement, the strength of the inference is greatly increased.

3.3 ISSUES IN DESIGNING RESEARCH

The major challenge in choosing a design is the issue of the cause-and-effect relationship. It is easily said by many students that an increase in pay increases the motivation of employees. The scientific question is: How do you know that increases in pay (X) cause motivation (Y)?

The implication here is that the internal validity of a research design is therefore very important.

You must know that the requirements for causality require that other factors be ruled out as rival explanations of an observed association between Y and X. Campbell and Stanley (1963) called this the problem of *internal validity*. If you want to generalize your findings, then you will face another challenge of *external validity*. External validity measures the extent to which sample results are generalizable to the entire target population, that is, the extent to which the research finding can be generalized to the larger population.

Issues to take into account when you want to in generalize your findings include the following.

- the representativeness of the sample you are working with
- reactive arrangements generalizable not only to large populations but to a real-life setting

Example:

After several months of sales promotion, sales figures went up over all. However, the student noted that the final sales were moderated by media events that took place after the sales promotion project was introduced. There was also the recognition that the government had removed the tax on the products being promoted.

Several factors have been identified that may jeopardise internal validity. The factors can be extrinsic or intrinsic.

Extrinsic factors refer to possible biases resulting from different recruitment of research participants to experiment and control groups. This selection factor creates initial differences between experimental and control groups.

Intrinsic factors are changes in individuals or units that occur during the study period. They can also come from changes in measurement instruments.

Campbell and Stanley (1963) identified the following threats to internal validity.

1. *History.* History effects refer to all events occurring during the time of the study that might affect the individual programmes or policy being studied and provide rival explanations for the changes in the dependent variable.

Example:

A student wants to study the impact of sales promotion on the level of sales. She structured the design as follows:

Independent   Dependent

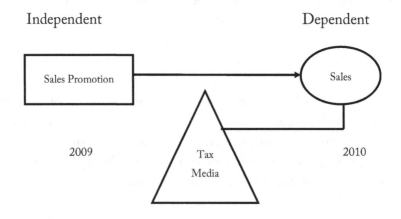

2. *Maturation.* These concerns include biological and psychological processes that produce changes in the individuals or units being studied.

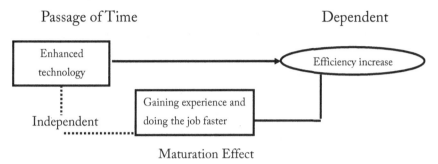

Maturation Effect

Example:

In this study, the government introduced computerised record keeping. After several years, an increase in the efficiency of record management was noted. The student found out that gaining experience with IT led to doing the job faster, which led to efficiency in performance.

Example:

In another ministry, IT was introduced in record keeping, but efficiency declined. The student found that in the latter case managers did not like using the IT. They had the technology, but they run parallel systems and preferred the old.

3. *Experimental Mortality.* This refers to drop-out problems during the research study. This may lead to a biased final sample selection. It prevents the collection of complete information.
4. *Instrumentation.* This refers to designated changes in the measurement instruments and pre-and post-tests.
5. *Testing.* The possible reaction to measurement is a real problem. The process of testing has been noted itself to change the phenomena being measured, such as a difference

between pre-and post-test. This would be attributed not to X but rather to the experience gained while taking the test.

6. *Regression Artefact.* This is the threat that occurs when individuals have been selected on the basis of extreme scores on the dependent variables.

7. *Interactions with Selection.* Many of the factors interact with selection and present added threats to the validity of the study.

3.4 *PROCEDURES FOR CONTROL*

When designing the study, you must endeavour to control factors that may threaten the validity of the causal reference you may make at the end of the study.

Below we present summaries of how the major extrinsic and intrinsic factors that threaten internal validity of causal inference can be controlled.

Matching. Matching is equating the experimental and control groups on extrinsic variables related to the hypothesis. Several studies use a common method of matching, that is, precision matching/pairwise matching. Using this method, for each case in the experimental group, another case with identical characteristics is selected for control group. Having matched on the extrinsic factor, you can conclude any difference in experimental and control group is not due to the matched variable.

Frequency Distribution. The experimental and control groups are made similar to each other on the relevant variables. For example, sex can be controlled by making sure that groups have the same proportions of male and female.

Randomization. Randomization is a process through which cases are assigned to the experimental and control groups. Randomization is accomplished using techniques such as flipping a coin, using a table of random digits, or making sure that all of the cases have an equal probability of being assigned to either the experimental or the control group.

It is noted that randomisation cancels out the effects of any systematic error due to extrinsic variables.

3.5 WHICH DESIGN?

In this chapter, you have seen that there are many issues you will have to consider when selecting a research design. Your research design "will be based on a flow of logic and a number of assumptions, all of which must stand up to the closest scrutiny" (Saunders 2007, p. 155). Please note the difference and specific requirements when you use experimental designs.

Most of you will end up using quasi-experimental designs. However, be sure that you note their weaknesses and their limitations.

CHAPTER FOUR

DATA COLLECTION METHODS

Having decided on the "what" and the "how" of the investigation, we then proceed to determine how you should go out and collect your data. It is important to know that not every data collection method will be appropriate for your study.

4.1 FORMS OF DATA COLLECTION

There are basically two types of data—primary and secondary data. Looking at past theses, three collection methods appear to be common.

1. *The Unstructured Interview.* You will have no list of predetermined questions. However, you need to have a clear idea about the aspect you want to explore (Saunders *et al.*, 2007). You will talk freely.

2. *The Semi-Structured Interview.* You will develop a list of themes and questions to be covered, but these questions may vary from interview to interview. Sometimes questions will vary depending on the level where the respondent is coming from in the organization. You will be good at note taking, or if acceptable, you may use a tape recorder.

3. *The Structured Interview.* You will construct predetermined and standardized questions. Usually, you can even create

pre-coded answers. You can read the question and record the answer from the respondent. You could also send the standardized questions by e-mail or post.

You must know that each form of interview has a distinct purpose. Saunders (2007, p. 303) identifies these purposes as follows.

1. Non-standardized interviews are used to gather data which is analysed qualitatively.
2. Standardized interviews are used to gather data which will then be the subject of quantitative analysis.

4.2 TYPES OF BEHAVIOUR TO OBSERVE

When designing data collection instruments, you will need to make some key decisions. The first is the decision on what you want to study. If you want to study the relationship between job satisfaction and performance, what exactly are you going to observe to measure "satisfaction" and the outcome "performance"? In your research methods course, some quality issues were identified when using semi-structured and in-depth interviews. So when you have selected those methods for collecting data, care must be taken to avoid response bias. To test this hypothesis, performance and job satisfaction need to be observed. So you require clear and precise operational definition of the two concepts. Some indicators of satisfaction and performance may include non-verbal expression, body movement, and extra-linguistic aspects.

4.3 SURVEY RESEARCH

Not all phenomena can be directly observed. You sometimes just want to ask people who have experienced certain phenomena to reconstruct these for you. This is done through interview. The most common interview modes are face-to-face and telephone. Internet interviews are also becoming common these days. Internet interviews are seen to provide advantages over other modes related to access, power, cost, and speed.

4.4 COLLECTING DATA THROUGH RESEARCH OBSERVATION

This method involves observing participants. Observation will include the observation, recording, analysis, and interpretation of events. There are basically different ways of participant observation. In some cases, the researcher participates in the lives and activities of the people being observed. Some of our students have written the study as "My Experience in This Organization." If you want to use this method, be careful, as it suffers from several threats to validity. The most common threat is observer bias. Kirkpatrick (1994, p. 43) said that "because we are part of the social world we are studying we cannot collect data on ourselves from it."

Table 4.1 shows the pros and cons of different primary data collection methods.

Table 4.1 A Comparison of Different Primary
Data Collection Methods

Criteria	Personal Interview	Mail	Telephone
Cost	High	Low	Moderate
Response rate	High	Low	High
Control of interview situation	High	Low	Moderate
Application to geographically dispersed population	Moderate	High	Moderate
Applicability to heterogeneous population	High	Low	High
Ability to obtain detailed information	High	Moderate	Moderate
Speed	Low	Low	High

4.5 COLLECTING SECONDARY DATA

In most cases you will also use secondary data in your study. There are some issues you need to sort out before you use such data. Secondary data is data already collected for some other purpose. We do have national census data, company accounting data, sales, global competitiveness data, corruption indices, etc.

Secondary data can be found either published or raw. Common sources of secondary data include documentaries and surveys. In many student thesis studies, both documentary and survey secondary data are used. Most students find secondary data useful when they are conducting a longitudinal study. However, secondary data should always be used with care, as this data was collected for a purpose other than your study.

Secondary data, however complex it maybe, if it does not help you answer your research questions, will result in invalid conclusions. (Kervin, 1999).

4.6 DESIGNING QUESTIONS

The foundation of all questionnaires is your research question. All the questions must translate the research objectives into specific questions. Answers to such research questions should provide the data for hypothesis testing.

There are several considerations to bear in mind when formulating questions. You must consider their content and structure and the format of the sequence of the questions.

4.6.1   Question Content

Are the questions concerned with facts or opinions and attitudes?

Factual questions are usually designed to elicit objective information. For example, all questions in the questionnaire concerning the respondent's background, environment, habits, experience, etc.

An example of a factual question is:

What is the last grade you attended? Please tick.

Primary

Secondary

University

Sometimes we can ask factual information about the respondent's social environment. For example:

Who are the people living with you in the household?
What means of transport do you use to go to work?
Are you self-employed?

Attitude and opinion questions are questions that refer to the sum total of inclinations, prejudices, ideas, fears, and convictions about a specific topic in your study. For example, you can ask your respondents about their opinions on HIV/AIDS. However, an attitude question about fighting against HIV/AIDS would provide a more general orientation of what a person feels and thinks about HIV/AIDS and its prevention.

Attitudes are described by their content—what they are about, their direction, whether they show positive, neutral, or negative feelings about the object or issue in question, and their intensity (greater or lesser vehemence).

We are interested in measuring attitudes because they account for general inclinations. So, how can we measure opinions and attitudes?

An opinion is generally measured by estimating what proportion of the surveyed population say they agree with a single statement of opinion. Attitudes are measured by attitude scales consisting of several attitude statements where respondents are asked to agree or disagree.

One essential requirement for attitude measurement is to use attitude statements. Such attitude statements can be scaled using attitude-scaling techniques. Attitudes and opinions do have varied aspects or dimensions, and respondents may sometimes agree with one aspect but disagree with another. Therefore, you may use several attitude statements to reduce one-sided responses.

4.6.2   Types of Questions

When you are designing the questions to be part of your questionnaire, remember there are three types of research questions. These include open-ended, closed, and contingent questions.

Closed questions offer a set of answers from which respondents choose one that closely represents their views.

Open-ended questions do not follow any kind of specified choice. Answers are recorded in full by the respondent.

Contingent questions are questions that follow some response to a closed question; they apply only to a sub-group of respondents. A contingent question is a follow-up question that is relevant and connected to the reply to the initial question.

Example:

Is this your first full time job?

Yes [ ]   No [ ]

If No, what happened to the job you held before:

Company folded   [ ]
Dismissed   [ ]
Didn't like it   [ ]

The standard format is to have a separate contingent question separate from an ordinary question to be answered by all.

Example:

Answer this question if you are a senior manager or else skip to question 10.

Did you take a college degree?

Yes   [ ]
No   [ ]

Then you follow with relevant questions for senior managers only.

Matrix Questions. A good questionnaire may also have matrix questions. These are used to organize a large set of rating questions. They have several response categories. Respondents are asked to agree or disagree with statements. Response categories typically include the following:

1. Strongly agree
2. Agree
3. Depends
4. Disagree
5. Strongly disagree

4.6.3   Structure and Sequence of Questions

Questions in the questionnaire should follow some logical format and must address all issues. Answers to questions will help you answer your research questions.

The sequencing of questions helps the respondent to follow the issues. The common tactic is to use the *funnel sequence*. The funnel sequence is whereby successive questions asked are related to the previous ones but have a progressively narrow scope.

An illustration of an inverted funnel sequence is as follows:

1.   How many people were killed in the accident?
2.   How many were seriously injured?
3.   How long did it take the ambulance to reach the spot?
4.   In general how well do you think first aid operations were done?.

4.6.4   Avoiding Pitfalls in Question Construction

When designing questions, be careful with the following:

- the wording of questions
- responses which tend to answer questions in a particular way regardless of the question's content
- leading questions
- threatening questions or questions that are embarrassing or difficult to answer
- double-barrelled questions where you ask two or more questions in one

4.7 ETHICS IN DATA COLLECTION

Ethics refers to the appropriateness of your behaviour as a researcher in relation to the rights of those who become the subject of your work or are affected by the work directly or indirectly.

Ethical issues relating to data collection methods usually include the following:

- treating information confidentially
- misrepresentation of information or data collected
- handling personal information
- misrepresentation or distortion in reporting
- physical or mental loss to the subjects
- forced participation in the research study
- debriefing techniques that are unethical

CHAPTER FIVE

SAMPLING PROCEDURES

5.1 THE NEED TO SAMPLE

In your research problem statement you will have described clearly the target research population. The target population comprises the whole collection of things or elements under consideration in your research study. Here are examples of target populations for study:

- a population of banks in Nairobi
- a population of rural farmers in the Arusha region of Tanzania
- a population of women entrepreneurs in Kampala
- a population of Chinese construction companies in East Africa
- a population of states in Southern Africa
- a population of beer consumers in Arusha Town
- a population of customers of Barclays Bank in Dar es Salaam
- a population of machines in a factory
- a population of invoices in an organization
- a population of employees in an organization
- a population of malaria patients in a district hospital

You need to decide if a population study or *census* or a sample survey will be required or not. A sample survey provides a valid alternative to a census for the following reasons (The Zimbabwe Society of Health, 2002):

1. *Destructive examination procedures.* Some procedures for examining population elements in a study can be destructive. In such cases, dealing with samples is the most reasonable and ethical alternative.

2. *Time and cost reduction.* In many cases, research focuses on such a large target population that, for practical reasons, it is only possible to include some of its members in the study. You have to draw a sample from the total population. Many research proposals would take too long to complete and the costs would be too high if censuses were done.

3. *Inaccessibility of population elements.* Reaching all the population elements may be difficult due to various factors. Sampling may be the only method available in dealing with populations whose elements are not all available for study.

4. *Comparable results.* Sampling is a suitable alternative to a census when it is increasingly evident that sample results in similar past studies were comparable or even superior to census results.

5.2 SAMPLING DESIGNS

There are two types of sampling designs available, namely:

- probability or random sampling
- non-probability or non-random sampling

In probability (or random) sampling, the main assumption made is that the probability of selecting the elements (sampling units) from the target population to go into the sample basket is known and is finite (or non-zero). In non-probability (or non-random) sampling, the probability of selecting the elements is not known.

Figure 5.1 Process of Sample Selection.

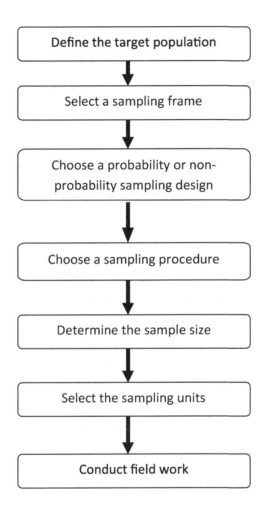

The stages in the sampling process are shown in Figure 5.1. The first step is to define your *target population*. What is your target population? What is its size? Where is it located? What are the main characteristics of the population?

The second step is to select the *sampling frame*. The sampling frame is a complete listing of all elements in the target population that are available for the study. The sampling frame is your working population for the study. Sampling frame examples might include:

- employee payroll at XYZ Company Ltd.
- the register of accountants registered with the Association of Accountants in Tanzania
- the list of commercial farmers registered with the Commercial Farmers Union in Zambia
- the list of banks registered with the Central Bank in Kenya

Where a suitable list exists, it is convenient to use it for your study. Where such a list does not exist, you will have to compile your own sampling frame. The sampling frame must be complete, unbiased, current, and accurate.

5.3   DETERMINATION OF SAMPLE SIZE (n)

You need to decide on the suitable sample size (*n*) that will be needed for your study. Leedy (1997) states that the sample size depends largely on the degree to which the sample approximates the qualities and characteristics of the general population. You will need a larger sample if the general population is heterogeneous than if the population is more homogeneous. Saunders *et al.* (2007), states that generalizations about populations from data collected using any probability sample are based on *probability*. The larger your sample size, the lower the likely error in generalizing to the whole population. Probability sampling is therefore a compromise between the accuracy of your findings and the amount of time and money you invest in collecting and analysing the data. You should consider the following questions in making any decision on the sample size.

1.   What degree of precision is required between the sample and the whole population? This factor is usually expressed as the *margin of error*. In business research, researchers are usually

content to estimate the population's characteristics to within plus or minus three to five per cent of their true values. This means that if fifty per cent of your sample is in a certain category, then your estimate for the total population within the same category will be fifty per cent plus or minus the margin of error.

2. What *confidence level* do you need to have in your data? What level of certainty will be needed in the sample characteristics for them to be representative of the characteristics of the whole population? In business research, a 95 per cent level of certainty is usually assumed. This means that if your sample was selected 100 times, at least 95 of these samples would be certain to represent the characteristics of the population.

3. What is the variability of the population? This is usually expressed as the *standard deviation*.

4. What type of data analyses will you carry out? What is the number of categories into which data will be subdivided? Most statistical techniques require a minimum threshold of data categories, e.g., χ^2 statistical analysis.

5. What is the population size?

6. What sampling method should be employed?

The minimum sample size (n) can be computed using the following formula (deVaus, 1991):

$$n = pq \left[\frac{z}{e}\right]^2$$

where: n is the minimum sample size required
p is the proportion belonging to the specified category
q is the proportion not belonging to the specified category
z is the confidence factor at the required confidence level
e is the margin of error required

If the confidence level and the margin of error are known, then it is relatively easy to estimate the proportion of responses you expect to have a particular attribute (*a%*). This is normally done by taking a pilot sample of thirty observations and from this inferring the likely proportion for the main survey. The methods used in the pilot must be used in the main survey. The proportion can also be obtained from similar past surveys. The *worst-case scenario* is to assume that fifty per cent of the sample will have the specified attribute.

The confidence factors are 1.65 at 90% level of confidence; 1.96 at 95% level of confidence; and 2.57 at 99% level of confidence.

deVous (1991) states that when your population is less than 10,000 elements, a smaller sample size (known as the *adjusted minimum sample size*) can be used without affecting the accuracy. The adjusted sample size (*n*) is computed using the following formula:

$$n' = n/(1 + (n/N))$$

where: *n'* is the adjusted minimum sample size
         n is the minimum sample size
         N is the total population size

Table 5.1 gives sample sizes for different population sizes at a 95% level of certainty (assuming data are collected from all cases in the sample).

Table 5.1 Sample Sizes Required for Given Population Sizes

Population (*N*)	Sample Size (*n*)			
	5% Margin of Error	3% Margin of Error	2% Margin of Error	1% Margin of Error
50	44	48	49	50
100	79	91	96	99
150	108	132	141	148
200	132	168	185	196
250	151	203	226	244

Table 5.1 (Continued)

300	168	234	267	291
400	196	291	334	384
500	217	340	414	475
750	254	440	571	696
1,000	278	516	706	906
2,000	322	696	1,091	1,655
5,000	357	879	1,622	3,288
10,000	370	964	1,936	4,899
100,000	383	1,056	2,345	8,762
1,000,000	384	1,066	2,395	9,513
10,000,000	384	1,067	2,400	9,595

Adapted from Saunders *et al.*, 2007.

Once the minimum sample size has been determined, you need to estimate the *actual sample size* (n^a). The actual sample size is a function of the minimum sample (n) and the *response rate* (*RR*), and can be computed using the following formula:

$$n^a = \frac{n \times 100}{RR}$$

where: n^a is the actual sample size
         n is the minimum sample size
         RR is the response rate (as a percentage)

The response rate arises from respondents refusing to respond to individual questions in an interview or questionnaire or refusing to respond to the entire interview or questionnaire. The *field response rate* should be computed and reported in the thesis as part of your field results.

Lynn et al. (2001), proposed the following formula for computing the *overall field response rate* (RR):

$$RR = \frac{(I + P)}{\{(I + P) + (R + NC + O) + \alpha UC + \beta UN\}}$$

73

where: I is the number of complete interviews or questionnaires
P is the number of partial interviews or questionnaires
R is number of refusals
NC is the number of non-contacts
O is the number of other non-responses
UC is the number of contacted unknown eligibles
UN is the number of non-contacts out of the unknown eligibles
α is the estimated proportion of contacted cases of unknown eligibility that are eligible
β is the estimated proportion of non-contacted cases of unknown eligibility that are eligible

Refusals are those respondents that were sampled but refused to respond to individual questions or to the entire interview or questionnaire. *Non-contacts* are those respondents that were sampled but for some reason were not reachable on the interview day. *Other non-responses* include sampled respondents who are not competent to complete a questionnaire due to illness, hospitalization, or language barriers. *Unknown eligibles* are sampled respondents who are unreachable on the interview day due to change of address, or are in an unsafe area, or are in a place inaccessible due to weather conditions, etc. α and β can be assumed to equal 1 for most surveys. deVaus (1996), suggest a simplified formula for calculating the response rate as follows:

$$RR = \frac{Total\ number\ of\ responses}{Total\ number\ in\ sample - (ineligibles + unreachables)}$$

During your sampling design, you will need to determine the actual sample size using a *design RR*. The design response rate should be obtained from similar past research done in your country. If there is no past research done in your country, then use similar research done in other neighbouring countries or in other parts of the world. Table 5.2 shows response rate reported by various researchers.

Table 5.2 Response Rates Reported by Researchers

Type of Study	Researcher(s)	Reported Response Rate (%)
Postal survey	Saunders et al., 2007	15-20
Postal survey	Healy, 1991	50
Postal survey	Owen and Jones, 1994	30
Face-to-face interviews	Healy, 1991	75
Questionnaire survey	Saunders et al., 2007	52
Questionnaire survey	Dillman, 1978	50-92
Telephone interviews	Dillman, 1978	73-99
Interviews	Kervin, 1992	50

5.4 PROBABILITY (RANDOM) SAMPLING PROCEDURES

Statistical probability (or random) sampling is a method of sampling in such a way that each member of the target population has a known probability of being selected into the sample (The Zimbabwe Society of Health, 2002). Probability sampling is most commonly associated with *survey-based research*, where you need to make inferences from your sample about a population to answer your research question(s) or to meet your research objectives (Saunders *et al.*, 2007). The process of probability sampling can be divided into four stages:

1. Identify a suitable sampling frame based on your research question(s) or objectives.
2. Decide on a suitable sample size.
3. Select the most appropriate sampling technique and select the sample.
4. Check that the sample is representative of the population.

Probability sampling is suitable for target populations of sizes of fifty and above (Henry, 1990). If the number of elements in a population is under fifty, it is advisable to carry out a population study (census).

The following general guidelines can be used in choosing the sample:

1. For quantitative research studies, the sample size can be determined using statistical formula as shown above.
2. For qualitative research studies, the sample size should be large enough to allow for some generalization and small enough to allow for some intensive study.
3. The larger the target population size, the smaller the percentage of the population needed to get a representative sample.
4. If the target population is less than 100 elements, there is no need to sample. You can carry out a census.
5. If the target population is around 500 elements, you need to sample 50% of the population.
6. If the target population id around 1,500 elements, you need to sample 20% of the population.
7. For target population sizes above 5,000, the population size is almost irrelevant and a sample size of about 400 will suffice.

When the sampling frame has been selected and the sample size determined, the next step is to choose an appropriate sampling technique or procedure. The main probability sampling techniques include the following:

-   simple random sampling
-   systematic random sampling
-   stratified sampling
-   cluster sampling

The main non-probability (or non-random) sampling techniques include the following:

-   convenience sampling
-   judgment or purposive sampling
-   quota sampling
-   snowball sampling

Non-probability sampling is appropriate in studies that are more or less qualitative, where you wish to obtain in-depth knowledge of a relatively small sample or a single case without necessarily wanting to generalize your results to the whole population, and where, instead of testable hypotheses, you have developed research questions only.

5.4.1 Simple Random Sampling Technique

The simple random sampling procedure assumes that every element in the sampling frame has an equal chance of being selected to be in the sample. The most common selection process is sampling without replacement, that is, you don't replace a selected element back into the sampling frame. You may use the table of random numbers or computer random number generators to obtain the required sample. Appendix 2 shows the table of random numbers generated using the Stat Trek online random number generator (Stat Trek, 2007). Use the following steps to select a simple random sample.

1. Prepare the sampling frame.
2. Label each element in the list with unique numbers, starting with 0 for the first element, then 1 for the second element, and so on.
3. Select the sampling units using the random number table until the desired sample size is reached.

Worked Example:

In a study of Nakumatt Supermarket customers in Nairobi, you have a target population of 9,000 customers who use the Nakumatt customer card for their daily purchases at the Nakumatt Lifestyle store. In the study you wish to find out what motivates the customers to use the card when making purchases at the store. You determine the required sample size at a 100% design response rate to be 370, and you decide to select the sample using simple random sampling from an existing listing of card holders obtained from the store's customer service department.

Since N = 9,000 is a four-digit number, the unique labels to be used for the elements will also be four-digit. The first unique label is 0000, the second is 0001, and so on, and the last element is given label 8999. Suppose you decide to read the random numbers row by row from the top row. The unique numbers you read from the random number table extract given below will be as follows:

8630, 3180, 1107, 0919, 1973, 9853, 7833, 6846, . . .

The selected elements will therefore be as follows:

8630, 3180, 1107, 0919, 1973, 7833, 6846, . . .

Note that the number 9853 had been left out as it outside the range.

Extract of Random Numbers from Appendix 2.

86 30 31 80 11 07 09 19 73 98 53 78 33 69 46 15 42 32 32 74 01 26 70
78 95 79 21 35 33 92 12 38 06 92 14 39 49 19 21 72 77 49 38 12 35 96
24 70 28 77 17 86 21 28 59 54 02 85 35 54 41 55 66 23 60 20 67 45 73
09 45 68 62 71 09 55 61 77 86 61 26 34 26 99 66 16 90 26 80 66 34
39 15 35 28 71 14 02 35 02 21 48 80 52 80 97 85 26 31 52 72 94 34 78
03 21 87 05 40 47

5.4.2   Systematic Random Sampling Technique

In systematic sampling, elements are selected at regular intervals (e.g. every k^{th} element) from the sampling frame. Follow the following steps to select a systematic random sample.

1. Prepare or select the sampling frame.
2. Label the elements with unique numbers, starting with 0 for the first element.
3. Compute the *sampling fraction (Sf)* using the formula:

$$Sf = \frac{\text{actual sample size}}{Population\ size} = \frac{1}{k}$$

4. Select the first element from the first k elements using random numbers.
5. From the first selected element, use the sampling fraction to select every k^{th} element until the sample size is reached.

Worked Example:

Suppose a systematic sample is to be selected from 1,500 MBA students at ESAMI. The actual sample size chosen is 300. The sampling fraction is calculated as follows:

$Sf = n_a/N = 500/1,500 = 1/5 = 1/k$

Select the first student from the first five in the sampling frame using random numbers. If number 0003 is selected, then subsequent selections will be 0008, 0013, 0018, and so on until the sample size of 300 is reached.

Although systematic sampling is relatively easier and quicker than simple random sampling, it has one drawback. Its weakness arises when you have periodic patterns in the sampling frame, for instance in the above example, suppose that every fifth student selected is female, then you will end up with an unrepresentative sample of women only.

5.4.3   Stratified Random Sampling Technique

Stratified random sampling is a sampling procedure whereby you obtain a representative sample from groups (strata) of population elements with common attributes (for example, female and make MBA students, urban and rural farmers, employees of different age groups). The sampling frame is effectively divided into groups or strata according to these attributes. The sample is selected from the strata using simple or systematic random sampling. You may decide to select a proportionate sample or a disproportionate sample. A *proportionate sample* is one whereby the number of elements selected in each stratum is proportional to the size of the stratum. That is, the same sampling ratio is used in all strata. A *disproportionate sample* is obtained when different sampling ratios are used in different strata. This allows for sampling more elements in strata with fewer elements.

Data from various strata is collected and combined for the whole target population. If the same sampling ration is used, then the total sample is self-weighted and can be treated in the same way as a simple or systematic sample. If different sampling ratios were used, you might have to decide on an appropriate weighting procedure, making data analysis a little more complex. Use the following steps in selecting a stratified sample.

1. Identify the target population (sampling frame).
2. Define the stratification attribute.
3. List the population elements according to the defined strata.
4. Label each element in each stratum with a unique number, starting with 0 for the first element.
5. Determine the desired sample size and decide whether a proportionate sample or a disproportionate sample is required.
6. Select the sample using either simple random sampling or systematic random sampling.

5.4.4   Cluster Sampling Technique

In situations where the population is large and dispersed over a wide geographical area, obtaining a simple random sample can be extremely challenging in terms of time and cost. A complete sampling frame may not exist or be difficult to obtain.

When a large population is spread across a large area, you may obtain a map of the area showing subdivisions and boundaries. You can then subdivide the area into smaller units or clusters. Each cluster must be as similar as possible. Within the clusters, the elements must be heterogeneous. Clusters are often geographical units such as provinces, regions, districts, counties, constituencies, city districts, villages, markets, hospitals, government ministries, schools, and so on. The following steps may be useful in cluster sampling.

1.   Identify the target population (sampling frame).
2.   Choose the cluster grouping for your population.
3.   Determine the desired sample size.
4.   List the clusters randomly.
5.   Label each cluster with a unique number, staring with 0 for the first in the list.
6.   Using random numbers, select the sample using the simple random sampling procedure.
7.   All elements in each cluster selected are used as units of observation.

Cluster sampling tends to be easy and cost-effective. Cluster validity is high when clusters are highly similar.

5.5   NON-PROBABILITY (NON-RANDOM) SAMPLING PROCEDURES

Non-probability (non-random) sampling designs make the assumption that the probability of selecting each member of the target population is unknown. This implies that the researcher can choose a sample which is not necessarily representative of the target population. Hence, the results obtained with non-probability sampling may not necessarily be generalizable to the whole population. It is up to the researcher to try to choose a sensible sample that is representative of the target population. Non-probability sampling may be handy in situations where there time and cost constraints prohibit using probability sampling.

5.5.1   Convenience Sampling Technique

The *convenience sampling* procedure (also known as *haphazard* or *accidental sampling*) involves collecting information from population members who are most conveniently available to provide the required information. This sampling procedure can be used to collect information quickly and efficiently. Convenience sampling is often used during the exploratory stages of research projects.

For example, if you wish to measure the image of Shoprite Supermarket in Dar es Salaam, you can employ convenience sampling by actually going to the Shoprite store and standing by the main entrance where you would collect information from shoppers walking in or out. Shoprite's customers can be conveniently found at the shop, nowhere else. Notice that the actual sample size may not be determined in advance, since you don't know how many shoppers will be willing to take your questions.

5.5.2   Judgment Sampling Technique

The *judgment sampling* procedure is one of the two most commonly used *purposive sampling* procedures. The other purposive sampling procedure is *quota sampling*. Judgment sampling involves collecting information from a specific target group that is well placed to have the information being sought within the population. You use your experience and judgment to select population members who have the appropriate characteristics required for your sample members.

For example, if you want to find out what it takes for people to obtain PhD's, then you would sample only those people who actually have a PhD.

5.5.3   Quota Sampling Technique

Quota sampling is the second type of purposive sampling. Quota sampling assigns a quota to each distinct group or stratum having some common attribute within the target population. This ensures that each group is adequately represented in the sample. The selection of sample members is done in a convenient manner; hence, the results are still not necessarily generalizable to the whole population.

For example, if you need a sample of twenty managers from Company X, which has eight per cent middle managers and twenty per cent top managers, then you would sample a quota of sixteen middle managers and four top managers.

Quota samples are essentially stratified samples selected without using random numbers (that is, selected non-randomly). Hence, quota sampling is not the same as stratified random sampling.

5.5.4   Snowball Sampling Technique

Snowball sampling, also known as *networking*, is a sampling procedure which can be used in phenomenological research studies where you have initially selected a desired sample using purposive sampling procedures, and for some reason you wish to collect information from additional members. You then seek the help of the selected members to identify additional members, since probably they belong to the same network.

For example, you are conducting a study of the impact of retrenchment in the public service, and you desire a sample of thirty retrenchees from the Ministry of Health, but you have managed to obtain a convenient sample of twenty people only. Since most of these retrenchees from this ministry know one another and perhaps continue to network well after the retrenchment exercise was done, you can ask some members of the twenty to identify the remaining ten that you can sample to obtain a complete sample.

Snowballing can also be used to obtain replacements in situations where you have attrition of sample members.

CHAPTER SIX

DATA ANALYSIS METHODS

6.1 INTRODUCTION TO DATA ANALYSIS METHODS

Data analysis is the ordering and structuring of data to produce knowledge (Howard and Sharp, 1983). The main function of data analysis is to communicate the value of research findings to the reader of the research report. Data analysis enables you to build your own skills for evaluating previous research analyses. The role of analysis is to supply evidence which justifies claims that the research changes belief or knowledge and is of sufficient value (The Zimbabwe Society of Health, 2002). This is done though ordering or structuring of data.

If you have chosen a deductive research approach in your research, you will have collected mostly *quantitative data* which will require some form of statistical analysis. On the other hand, if you have chosen an inductive research approach, you will have collected mostly *qualitative data* which will require some qualitative technique to analyse. Phenomenological research can also generate quantitative data which will not require statistical analysis.

Quantitative data can be analysed using the following statistical techniques.

1. *Descriptive statistics,* where you just summarise or display quantitative data.
2. *Inferential statistics,* where you estimate unknown population parameters using sample numerical data or where you test hypotheses about population parameters and characteristics using sample data.

Hussey and Hussey (1997), state that the choice of a statistical technique will largely depend on the available time, cost, and access to a suitable computer software (Statistical Package for the Social Sciences SPSS, Minitab, or MS-Excel), and the following criteria.

1. Do you wish to conduct exploratory data analysis to summarise, describe, or display your data or confirmatory data analysis to make inferences from your sample data?
2. Does your data has a *normal distribution* which allows you to use the more powerful *parametric techniques* or is *skewed,* which means that you will have to use a *non-parametric technique?*
3. What is the *number of variables* you wish to analyse at the same time?
4. What is the measurement *scale* of your data (*nominal, ordinal, interval, or ratio*), which has implications if you decide to use an *inferential technique?*

Sekaran (2003) identifies three objectives of data analysis.

*   getting a feel for the data
*   testing the goodness of data
*   testing the hypotheses or answering the research questions developed for the study

Before the above steps can be executed, data need to be prepared for analysis.

6.2 *PREPARING DATA FOR ANALYSIS*

Data collected with questionnaires, interviews, or structured observation should be edited for accuracy and consistency. This should be done on the same day the data has been obtained in order to be able to conduct follow-ups with the respondents.

Some questionnaires may have to be discarded if many questions have been left uncompleted by a respondent. The rule of thumb is that if twenty-five per cent or more of the questions in a questionnaire have not been answered, then the questionnaire should be discarded since it is ineligible. Determination of the final response rate (*RR*) should take into account such ineligible questionnaires.

If fewer than twenty-five per cent of the questions are unanswered in a questionnaire, then a way should be found of handling the blank responses. Sekaran (2003), suggests the following ways of handling blank responses to interval-scaled items,

1. Assign the scale mid-point to that blank item.
2. Allow the computer to ignore the blank response when analysing the data.
3. Assign to the blank the mean value of the responses of all those who have responded to that particular item.
4. Assign to the missing item the mean of the responses to all other questions measuring the same variable in the questionnaire.
5. Assign to the missing response a random number within the scale.

Responses in a questionnaire should then be coded for ease of data entry on a computer. For example, consider the following question.

Q. Your sex. Please tick. 1. F [ ] 2. M [ ]

The numbers [1] and [2] can be used as codes and entered on the computer for analysis.

Before data can be entered on a computer, items measuring the same variable need to be *categorised* or grouped together for ease of analysis later on.

Data can be entered in a computer spreadsheet such as MS-Excel or a statistical package such as SPSS. Columns in the data field are used as the variables, and the rows can represent the elements.

6.3 GETTING A FEEL FOR THE DATA

Before you can apply any sophisticated statistical analysis to your data, you need to have "a feel for the data". This refers to an initial impression of the data and an impression of the underlying distribution of data values. A feel for the data will guide you to select appropriate statistical techniques in subsequent analyses.

A feel of the data can be achieved by computing the following descriptive statistical measures.

- measures of central tendency, including the arithmetic mean, the median, and the mode
- measures of variation or dispersion, including the range, the mean deviation, the variance, the standard deviation, and the coefficient of variation
- frequency distributions
- regression and correlation analysis

Statistical *measures of central tendency and variation* provide an impression of how the data is spread from a central point. If the variation is large, it means the underlying distribution of data values is more or less non-uniform. If the variation is small, it means the underlying distribution of data values is more or less uniform. These statistical measures should be computed for both dependent and independent variables. *Frequency distributions* will also show whether the underlying distribution of data values is uniform or not. *Regression analysis* involves establishing a mathematical equation to describe a relationship between two or more variables. *Correlation analysis* provides an impression of the strength between two or more variables. Obtain an inter-correlation matrix for all variables. A large correlation coefficient (>0.5) between two variables would mean a strong relationship between variables.

6.4   TESTING FOR GOODNESS OF DATA

In order to test the reliability of the measures, you should compute the Cronbach's alpha (α). Cronbach's alpha estimates the reliability of a measuring instrument or scale by determining the internal consistency of the instrument or the average correlation of the items measuring the same variable (Cronbach, 1951).

The Cronbach's α can be computed using the following formula:

$$\alpha = \frac{N \cdot \bar{r}}{(1 + (N - 1) \cdot \bar{r})}$$

Where: N is the number of components (items)
$\bar{r}$ is the average of all Pearson correlation coefficients between the components or items.

Cronbach's alpha values are interpreted as shown in Table 6-1.

Table 6.1 Interpretation of Cronbach's Alpha Values

Cronbach's Apha Value	Level of Internal Consistency
$a = 1.0$	Too good to be true! Look at the questions—they must be identical.
$0.9 \leq a < 1.0$	Excellent
$0.8 \leq a < 0.9$	Good
$0.7 \leq a < 0.8$	Acceptable
$0.6 \leq a < 0.8$	Questionable
$0.5 \leq a < 0.6$	Poor—You really do not have a scale; stick to the items.
$a < 0.5$	Unacceptable—You really do not have a scale; stick to the items.

6.5 TESTING HYPOTHESES

The choice of a statistical test of hypothesis depends on the following factors.

1. The type of research question to be answered. A given research question will determine the choice of a given statistical technique.
2. The number of variables investigated simultaneously. *Univariate data analysis* is done on a single variable only. *Bivariate data analysis* is conducted on data collected on a pair of variables. *Multivariate data analysis* is done on more than two variables.
3. The scale of measurement employed. Data collected on an interval and a ratio scale will require testing hypothesis about a mean using either the Z-test (if the sample size is large, i.e., $n \geq 30$) or the t-test (if the sample size is small, i.e., $n < 30$). Data collected on an ordinal scale and a nominal scale will require testing a hypothesis using the χ^2 test.

The following seven steps should be followed in testing hypotheses in both parametric and non-parametric tests.

1. Formulate your hypotheses, the Null hypothesis, and the Alternate hypothesis.
2. Set the alpha (α)-level of significance, typically at α = 0.05 for business research studies.
3. Determine the critical values.
4. Compute the test statistic using an appropriate formula.
5. Compare the value of the test statistic and the critical value(s).
6. Come to a conclusion to reject or not to reject the Null hypothesis
7. Put your conclusion in English.

Common parametric tests requiring data to be collected on either an interval or ratio scale include the following:

*   Pearson's product moment correlation coefficient
*   Standard Normal Z-tests
*   Student t-tests
*   ANOVA test

Common non-parametric tests requiring data to be collected on an ordinal or nominal scale include the following.

*   the χ^2 test
*   Spearman's rank correlation coefficient:

CHAPTER SEVEN

SOME STATISTICAL TECHNIQUES IN RESEARCH

7.1 INTRODUCTION

A feel for the data can be achieved by computing the following descriptive statistical measures:

- frequency distributions
- measures of central location/tendency, including the arithmetic mean, the median, and the mode
- measures of variation or dispersion, including the range, the mean deviation, the variance, the standard deviation, and the coefficient of variation
- regression and correlation analysis

7.2 FREQUENCY DISTRIBUTION

A *frequency distribution* is a table in which possible values for a variable are grouped into classes (or class intervals), and the number of observed values which fall into each class is recorded. This frequency distribution is called a *grouped frequency distribution*. A *simple or discrete frequency distribution* consists of a list of data values, each showing the number of items having that value (i.e., the frequency).

Simple frequency distributions are constructed for discrete raw data (i.e., data measured by counting). Frequency distributions are usually constructed with the help of *tally marks*.

Example: Computing a Simple Frequency Distribution

Here is a worked example of calculating a simple frequency distribution.

Compile a simple frequency distribution for the following data using a tally chart. The data represent the number of children in the families of forty-seven workers at ESAMI.

113 202 012 213 524 002 411 220
300 213 602 103 222 100 113 14

Answer:

The tally chart and the resultant simple frequency distribution are given in Table 7.1.

Table 7.1 Simple (Discrete) Frequency Distribution

Data Value	Tally Marks	Total	Frequency, f_i (Number of workers)
0	IIII IIII I	11	11
1	IIII IIII II	12	12
2	IIII IIII III	13	13
3	IIII I	6	6
4	III	3	3
5	I	1	1
6	I	1	1

Interpretation:

We can make statements such as, "There are twelve workers having one child in their families."

A *grouped frequency distribution* is constructed for data values that are continuous in nature (not discrete) and when there are more than thirty in a data set (or sample). It summarises values into groups or classes of values, each showing the number of items having values in the group. A tally chart can also be used to summarise the data observations.

Example: Computing a Grouped Frequency Distribution

The number of orders received each week over a period of forty weeks by Digital Computers Limited, a company based in Arusha, Tanzania, is given in Table 7.2. With the aid of tally marks, construct a grouped frequency distribution.

Table 7.2 Number of Orders Received Each Week
at Digital Computers Limited

24	13	28	15	25	29	15	46
9	10	17	22	23	17	16	32
11	12	18	20	13	27	18	22
20	14	26	14	19	19	40	31
17	21	23	26	18	24	21	27

Answer:

Table 7.3 A Grouped Frequency Distribution
of the Number of Orders Received
Each Week at Digital Computers Limited

Class interval (Number of orders)	Tally marks	Frequency, f_i (Number of weeks)
5 but under 10			1
10 but under 15	|||| ||	7
15 but under 20	|||| |||| |	11
20 but under 25	|||| ||||	10
25 but under 30	|||| ||	7
30 but under 35	||	2
35 but under 40		0
40 but under 45			1
45 but under 50			1
	Total:	$40 = \Sigma f = n$

Interpretation:

We can make statements such as, "During the forty-week period, there are eleven weeks having orders that lie in the range of fifteen to twenty."

Note that the sum of the class frequencies (f_i) equals the data set (sample) size, *n*.

7.3   THE ARITHMETIC MEAN

The *arithmetic mean* is the most popular *measure of central location or central tendency* of a distribution of data values. The arithmetic mean is the arithmetic average of item values in a data set or sample. It is computed as the sum of all item values divided by the number of item values in a data set.

For discrete data, the arithmetic mean is computed using the following formula.

$$\bar{X} = \frac{\sum x_i}{n}$$

$$\mu = \frac{\sum x_i}{N}$$

where: $\bar{X}$ is the sample mean
x denotes item values in the sample data set
i denotes is a counter from 1 to n
n denotes the number of item values in the data set
μ is the population mean
N is the population size

For grouped data, the arithmetic mean for *n* values in a data set is given by the following formula.

$$\bar{X} = \frac{\sum f_i x_i}{\sum f_i}$$

where: $\bar{X}$ is the sample mean
x denotes item values in the sample data set
i denotes is a counter from 1 to *j*
j denotes the number of class intervals

Example: Computing the Arithmetic Mean for Discrete Data

The data in Table 7.4 relates to a sales representative's weekly commission over seven consecutive weeks.

Table 7.4 Weekly Commission Data

Week Number:	1	2	3	4	5	6	7
Commission (TShs '000):	42	36	39	38	40	34	32

Substituting the figures in the formula, we get the following answer.

$$\overline{X} = \frac{TShs\ 261{,}000}{7} = TShs\ 37{,}286.$$

The interpretation of this result is that the commission of TShs 37,286 is a typical figure about which all the weekly commissions cluster.

Example: Computing the Arithmetic Mean for Grouped Data

The data in Table 7.5 shows to the number of successful sales in a particular quarter made by the salesmen employed by DK Computers, a large computer firm in Lusaka. Calculate the mean of the sales.

Table 7.5 Number of Successful Sales at DK Computers

Number of Sales:	0-4	5-9	10-14	15-19	20-24	25-29
Number of Salesmen:	1	14	23	21	15	6

To determine the average number of sales, you need to take the mid-points of the class intervals and multiply them by the class frequencies as shown in Table 7.6.

Table 7.6 Computation of the Mean for Grouped Data:
Number of Sales

No. of Sales	No. of Salesmen (f_i)	Mid-Point (x_i)	($f_i X_i$)
0-4	1	2.5	2.5
5-9	14	7.5	105
10-14	23	12.5	287.5
15-19	21	17.5	367.5
20-24	15	22.5	337.5
25-29	6	27.5	165
Total:	80		1265

Substituting the figures in the formula, the mean number of sales is:

$$\overline{X} = \frac{\Sigma f_i x_i}{\Sigma f_i} = \frac{1,265}{80} = 15.8 \text{ sales}$$

The advantages of using the arithmetic mean as a measure of central location or central tendency are as follows.

1. The arithmetic mean can be computed exactly.
2. The arithmetic mean is representative of all data values.
3. The arithmetic mean can be used in other more sophisticated statistical calculations.

The disadvantages of the arithmetic mean are as follows.

1. The arithmetic mean is a misleading measure of central location when data values contain extreme values (outliers).
2. It can provide a meaningless figure when the data values are discrete; for example, an arithmetic mean of 20.6 MBA students in class.

7.4 THE MEDIAN

The *median* is a robust measure of central location, since it is not affected by extreme data values in a sample. The median is the mid-value in a frequency distribution which has been arranged in size order. In other words, the median is the value below which half the values in the sample fall. The following formula can used to locate the position of the median value in a size-ordered distribution of data values.

$$\text{Median position} = \frac{n+1}{2}$$

where: n is the number of data values in the sample

See the example below using the commission data given in Table 7.4.

Example: Computing the Median for Ungrouped Data

Table 7.8 shows the size-ordered commission data of Table 7.4. There are seven data values in the sample ($n = 7$).

Table 7.8 Size-Ordered Commission Data

Week Number:	7	6	2	4	3	5	1
Commission (TShs '000):	32	34	36	38	39	40	42

$$\text{Median position} = \frac{n+1}{2} = \frac{7+1}{2} = 4$$

The median value is therefore the fourth data value (= TShs 38,000) in the size-ordered sample. Clearly, this is the mid-value in the size-ordered data set in Table 7.8. In the case of an even number of observations, the median position falls in between the two middle observations of a size-ordered data set. The median value in this case is the arithmetic mean of the middle two observations.

The median for grouped data can be computed using an interpolation formula and graphical interpolation (see Francis, 2004).

Using the median as a measure of central location has the following advantages.

1. The median is robust, as it is not affected by extreme data values.
2. The median is robust, as it is not affected by open-ended classes and irregular class sizes.
3. The median can represent an actual data value in the sample.
4. The median can be determined even if some data values are unknown in the sample.

The median has the following disadvantages.

1. For grouped frequency distributions of data values, the median can only be determined by estimation.
2. Once computed, the median cannot be used in subsequent statistical calculations.
3. For irregular (non-uniform) distributions, the median may not be representative of the distribution.

7.5 THE MODE

The *mode* is the data value that occurs with the highest frequency. It is a measure of central location in terms of being the most "popular" data value in a sample or data set.

Example: Computing the Mode for Ungrouped Data

Table 7.9 shows head sizes of factory workers at Maendeleo Metal Works in Nairobi. You have been hired to advise management at

Maendeleo Metal Works in on the appropriate helmet size for its workers.

Table 7.9 Head Sizes of Factory Workers at Maendeleo

Employee Code:	1	2	3	4	5	6	7	8	9
Head Size (in Inches):	6	6.5	7	7	7	7.5	8	8.5	9

From the data set in Table 7.9, the most common head size is 7 inches. This is the mode. The median head is also 7 inches, while the mean head size is 7.38 inches (which is close to 7.5 inches). Hence, if you chose a helmet having the mode (or median) size of 7 inches, it would fit three workers exactly. On the other hand, if you chose a helmet of size 7.5 inches, it would fit only one worker.

Example: Computing the Mode for Grouped Data

In order to determine the mode of grouped data (frequency distributions), first of all we have to determine the modal class. The modal class is the one with the highest frequency. The mode lies within the modal class interval. The mode is computed using the following formula.

$$\text{The Mode} = LCB + \left\{ \frac{f_1 - f_0}{2f_1 - f_0 - f_2} \right\} X\, h$$

where: LCB = lower class boundary of the modal class
f_1 = frequency of the modal class
f_0 = frequency of the class preceding the modal class
f_2 = frequency of the class succeeding the modal class
h = the class size

Consider the grouped data in Table 7.5.

$LCB = 9.5$ $f_1 = 23$ $f_0 = 14$ $f_2 = 21$ $h = 5$

The mode = 9.5 + {(23 - 14)/(2x23 - 14 - 21)}x 5 = 13.6 sales.

The mode has the following advantages as a measure of central location.

1.   The mode is a robust measure of central location, since it is not affected by extreme values in a data set.
2.   The mode is easy to compute even for grouped data.
3.   For grouped data, only frequency values within the modal class interval are used for the calculation.

The mode has the following disadvantages as a measure of central location.

1.   A data set or distribution may contain more than one mode.
2.   The mode cannot be determined exactly for grouped data.
3.   The mode is unstable, and it can change with more data items.
4.   The mode cannot be used in subsequent statistical computations.

7.6   THE RANGE

The *range* is the simplest *measure of variation or dispersion* of a distribution of data values. Measures of variation describe the extent to which data values in a distribution are spread or scattered. The spread can be determined overall or with respect to a central location value, for example, the arithmetic mean.

The range is computed as the difference between the largest and the smallest data values in a distribution.

Range = Largest value - Smallest value

Example: Computing the Range

Table 7.10 shows the daily number of rejected items detected from the separate output of two industrial machines over fourteen days.

Table 7.10 Daily Industrial Machine Rejects

Day:	1	2	3	4	5	6	7	8	9	10	11	12	13	14
Machine 1:	4	7	1	2	2	6	2	3	0	4	5	3	7	4
Machine 2:	3	2	2	3	3	2	4	1	1	3	2	4	2	2

The range for Machine 1 = 7 - 0 = 7
The range for Machine 2 = 4 - 1 = 3

Note that in order to find or compute the range, one needs to arrange the data in an array form or order of magnitude.

The above results show that the spread or variation of rejects over the 14-day period is larger in Machine 1.

The advantages of the range are as follows.

1.   The range is very simple to compute.
2.   The range can be used for quality control purposes. Small samples of output can be taken at regular intervals, and the range can be recorded for the samples over time. The range can thus provide a quick and easy check of production variability.

The major disadvantages of the range are as follows.

1.   The range is not a representative measure of variation in that it is computed using only two data values in a given data set, ignoring all other intermediate data values.

2.   The range has no natural partner in a measure of central location to be used together in subsequent statistical computations.

7.7. *THE MEAN DEVIATION*

The *mean deviation* is a measure of variation that gives the average absolute difference between each data value and the arithmetic mean for a given data set. The mean deviation is a much more representative measure of variation than the range, because its computation takes account of each and every data value in a data set.

The mean deviation *MD* is computed using the following formula for ungrouped data values.

$$MD = \frac{\sum |x_i - \bar{x}|}{n}$$

For grouped data the mean deviation is computed using the following formula.

$$MD = \frac{\sum f_i |x_i - \bar{x}|}{\sum f_i}$$

where all symbols have their usual meaning.

The symbol comprising two vertical lines is called the *modulus* function. The modulus function always outputs a positive result, even when the answer inside is negative.

Example: Computing the Mean Deviation

Suppose an MBA student obtained the following marks in four examinations she sat during one semester: 50, 85, 90, 55.

Then, the mean is: $\bar{x} = \frac{280}{4} = 70$

The mean deviation is therefore:

$$MD = \frac{|50-70|+|85-70|+|90-70|+|55-70|}{4} = \frac{70}{4} = 17.5$$

7.8 THE VARIANCE AND STANDARD DEVIATION

The *variance* is a measure of variation similar to the mean deviation in that it measures variation with respect to the arithmetic mean of data vales. Instead of taking the absolute value of the difference between a data value and the mean, we take the square of the deviations.

The *variance* S^2 for ungrouped data is computed using the following formula.

$$S^2 = \frac{\Sigma(x_i-\bar{x})^2}{n}$$

For grouped data, the variance is computed using the following formula.

$$S^2 = \frac{\Sigma f_i(x_i - \bar{x})^2}{\Sigma f_i}$$

where all symbols have their usual meaning.

The variance has the problem of squaring the units of measurement in the end result. In order to obtain the original units, it is obvious that we need to take a square root of the variance. The square root of the variance gives one of the most popular measures of variation computed in research, the standard deviation.

The formula for computing the standard deviation is given by the following formula,.

$$S = \sqrt{\frac{\Sigma(x_i - \bar{x})^2}{n}}$$

where all symbols have their usual meaning.

For grouped data, the standard deviation is computed using the following formula.

$$S = \sqrt{\frac{\Sigma f_i(x_i - \bar{x})^2}{\Sigma f_i}}$$

where all symbols have their usual meaning.

Example: Computing the Standard Deviation

Using the MBA student marks data above, the standard deviation is calculated as follows.

$$S = \sqrt{\frac{(50 - 70)^2 + (85 - 70)^2 + (90 - 70)^2 + (55 - 70)^2}{4}} = 17.7$$

Notice that the standard deviation result is almost equal to the mean deviation result.

7.9 *REGRESSION AND CORRELATION ANALYSIS*

Regression analysis involves obtaining a mathematical equation that describes the relationship between two variables or characteristics. The variables are typically the dependent variable and the independent variable. The equation can be used to predict values of the dependent variable for any given values of the independent variable. If the independent variable is a time variable, prediction is the same as forecasting. Regression equations can therefore be used to forecast future values of the dependent variable.

The y on x regression equation is of the following form.

$$y = mx + c$$

where y is the dependent variable
         x is the independent variable
         m is the gradient or rate of change in y with respect to unit change in x
         c is the intercept

The values m and c are the unknown numeric constants. Once the unknown numeric constants m and c are determined, then the equation is also determined. The gradient and the intercept are computed using the following formula.

$$m = \frac{n \sum xy - \sum x \sum y}{n \sum x^2 - (\sum x)^2}$$

$$c = \frac{\sum y}{n} - m \frac{\sum x}{n}$$

EXAMPLE: Obtaining a Linear Regression Equation

Table 7.11 shows the number of calls made by a salesman during an eight-week period and the corresponding number of orders taken. Obtain a regression equation showing the relationship between the number of orders taken and the number of calls made by the salesman.

Table 7.11 Sales Data Gathered by a Salesman

Week	Number of Calls	Number of Orders
1	10	1
2	14	2
3	12	2
4	20	4
5	18	3
6	20	6
7	26	8
8	24	6

Your aim therefore is to fit a regression equation

$$y = mx + c$$

This is done by computing m and c using the using the regression formulae.

$$m = \frac{n \sum xy - \sum x \sum y}{n \sum x^2 - (\sum x)^2}$$

$$c = \frac{\sum y}{n} - m \frac{\sum x}{n}$$

First, we need to compute the summations as shown in Table 7.12.

Table 7.12 Computing Summations for the Sales Data

Week	Number of calls (x)	Number of orders (y)	(xy)	x^2	y^2
1	10	1	10	100	1
2	14	2	28	196	4
3	12	2	24	144	4
4	20	4	80	400	16

Table 7.12 (Continued)

5	18	3	54	324	9
6	20	6	120	400	36
7	26	8	208	676	64
8	24	6	144	576	36
Sum:	144	32	668	2,816	170

Computing the gradient,

$$m = \frac{(8)(668)-(144)(32)}{8(2,816)-(144)^2} = 0.41$$

$$c = \frac{32}{8} - (0.41)\frac{144}{8} = -3.4$$

The number of orders y on the number of calls x regression equation is therefore given by: the following.

$$y = 0.41x - 3.4$$

We can use this equation to predict the number of orders for any given number of calls. For example, when the number of calls is 30, they will attract about 9 orders, and 100 calls will attract about 38 orders, etc.

Now, how do we know that our regression equation is good enough for predicting the number of orders? The obvious answer is: "We cannot know." We therefore need to determine the strength of the relationship expressed by the regression equation. This is where correlation analysis is needed.

The *Pearson's product moment correlation coefficient* r_p provides a measure of the strength of association between two variables. The formula for computing r_p is as follows.

$$r_p = \frac{\Sigma xy - \frac{\Sigma x \Sigma y}{n}}{\sqrt{\left[\Sigma x^2 - \frac{(\Sigma x)^2}{n}\right]\left[\Sigma y^2 - \frac{(\Sigma y)^2}{n}\right]}}$$

where: y is the dependent variable
        x is the independent variable
        n is the sample size

Example: Determining the Strength of Association

How strong is the relationship between the two variables in our regression equation above? In other words, how good is our regression equation for predicting purposes?

Using computations done in Table 7.12, let us compute Pearson's product moment correlation coefficient.

$$r_p = \frac{668 - \frac{(144)(32)}{8}}{\sqrt{\left[2{,}816 - \frac{(144)^2}{8}\right]\left[170 - \frac{(32)^2}{8}\right]}} = 0.95$$

How do we interpret the result? When $r_p = 1$, this represents a perfect positive linear relationship (association) between the two variables; $r_p = -1$ represents a perfect negative linear relationship; and $r_p = 0$ represents the lack of a linear relationship or association between the variables. Therefore, an $r_p = 0.95$ means that there is a very strong positive association between the number of calls made by the salesman and the number of orders taken.

The next question which needs to be asked is "What is the statistical significance of the result?" To answer this question, we need to look up the appropriate critical value in the correlation coefficient table (see Appendix 3). An $r_p = 0.95$ is greater than the critical value of 0.549 (one-tail test) and also greater than the critical value of 0.632 (two-tail test). Testing the hypothesis that there is a (strong) relationship against the alternative that the opposite is true demands a two-tail test. We therefore conclude that the result is statistically significant at a five per cent level.

7.10 TECHNIQUES FOR TESTING HYPOTHESES

After presenting descriptive statistics, you may proceed to present inferential statistics. Inferential statistics are used when conducting confirmatory data analysis as follows:

- estimating from samples
- measuring the association between two or more variables
- measuring the difference between two or more variables

Inferential statistics are used to estimate (unknown) population parameters and to test hypotheses. Hypothesis tests can be parametric (done on metric data) or non-parametric (done on non-metric data). Another way of looking at this is that parametric tests are done on variables with a known distribution, while non-parametric tests are done on variables which are said to be distribution-free or whose distributions are unknown.

Parametric tests measure the statistical significance between the parameter of interest and a known test statistic. Parametric tests are more appropriate for data collected using the interval and ratio scale, and also when the sample size is large.

Common parametric tests requiring data to be collected on either an interval or ratio scale include the following:

- Standard Normal Z-tests
- Student t-tests

The most common non-parametric test requiring data to be collected on a nominal scale is the χ^2 test.

7.10.1 Hypothesis-Testing Procedure

The general approach to hypothesis testing is as follows:

1. Define a simple precise statement about the situation (the hypothesis), i.e., define a statistical hypothesis—the Null hypothesis, H_0. Also define the Alternative hypothesis, H_1, which is opposite to the Null.
2. Take a sample from the target population and compute the appropriate sample statistic.
3. Test this sample to see whether it supports the hypothesis or whether it makes the hypothesis highly improbable, i.e., compare the sample statistic value and the expected population parameter if the statistical hypothesis were true.
4. If the hypothesis is highly improbable, then reject it, otherwise accept it.

The *decision rule or criterion* for accepting or rejecting the Null hypothesis is called the *level of significance*, denoted by the Greek letter alpha (α). The level of significance is a critical probability in choosing between the Null hypothesis and the Alternative hypothesis. The level of significance determines the probability level, say $\alpha = 0.5$ or $\alpha = 0.01$, that is to be considered too low to warrant support of the Null hypothesis. On the assumption that the Null hypothesis being tested is true, if the probability of occurrence of the observed data is smaller than the level of significance, then the data suggest that the Null hypothesis should be rejected. This means there is evidence to support the contradiction of the Null hypothesis, meaning that the Alternative hypothesis is true.

7.10.2 Type I and Type II Errors

Statistical hypothesis testing is based on the theory of probability. In testing the Null hypothesis, there is always a finite chance of making a mistake. There are two types of errors that can be committed in hypothesis testing. Table 7.13 summarises the possible situations of making the two types of errors.

Table 7.13 Type I and Type II Errors in Hypothesis Testing

Decision	Null Hypothesis H_0 Is:	
	True	False
Do not Reject	Correct Decision	Type II error
Reject	Type I error	Correct Decision

The decision to reject a true H_0 leads to a Type I error, and the decision not to reject H_0 leads to a Type II error. The probability of making a Type I error is equal to α, the level of statistical significance. The probability of making a Type II error is denoted by the Greek letter beta, β. In business problems, Type I errors are generally seen to be more serious than Type II errors, and thus there is greater concern with determining the α-level of significance than the β-level.

7.10.3 Choosing the Appropriate Hypothesis Test

A researcher can interpret data in a number of ways. The appropriate hypothesis test will depend on a number of factors, namely:

- the type of research questions to be answered
- the number of variables delineated for measurement
- the scale of measurement employed

The *type of research question to be answered* will determine the choice of a statistical technique. For instance, a researcher may be concerned with the central location of a distribution or about the overall distribution of the variable. For example, a comparison of two departments' average sales (for a small sample, n ≤ 30) will require a Student t-test of two means, whereas a comparison of the quarterly sales values over a year's period will require a χ^2 test.

The *number of variables* that will be investigated at the same time is a primary consideration in the choice of a statistical technique. Analysis on a single variable (i.e., *univariate data analysis)* is conducted when a researcher wishes to generalize from a sample about one variable at a time—for example, an analysis of the relationship between Gross Domestic Product (GDP) and sales volume of an agricultural commodity at one given time.

Describing the relationship between two variables will require *bivariate data analysis*—for example, testing the association between the gender of beer drinkers and the alcoholic strength of the beer.

The *scale of measurement* on which the data are based will determine the statistical techniques to be employed by a researcher. Parametric tests will require data measured on an interval or ratio scale. On the other hand, non-parametric tests will require data measured on the nominal and ordinal scale.

7.10.4   Steps in Hypothesis Testing

There are seven steps in hypothesis testing. The steps are as follows:

- Step 1: State the hypothesis to be tested. The Null hypothesis is always assumed to be true.
- Step2: State the significance level.
- Step 3: State the critical values.
- Step 4: Calculate the test statistic.
- Step 5: Compare the test statistic value and the critical value.
- Step 6: Come to a conclusion, either to reject H_0 or not.
- Step 7: Put your conclusion into English.

7.10.5   The Z-Test of Hypothesis

The standard Normal or Z-test is a common parametric test in research. It can be conducted on one-sample data or on independent two-sample data. The Z-test is always conducted on data collected on *sample sizes greater than 30.*

Example: Z-test for One Sample

A store manager believes that the average amount spent on jam and marmalade is $1.50. A random sample of eighty shoppers was selected from a large population and tested about the amount spent per week on these items.

Results from the survey showed that the average amount spent per week in these areas was $1.40 with a standard deviation of $0.15. Does this lend support to the manager's opinion at the 5% significance level?

Answer:

Step 1: State the hypothesis, H_0 and its H_1.

> H_0 is such that the average amount spent on jam and marmalade is $1.50.
> H_1 is such that the amount spent is not equal to $1.50.
> Using statistical notation (two-tail test):
> $H_0: \mu = \$1.50$
> $H_1: \mu \neq \$1.50$

Step2: State the significance level.

> Choose $\alpha = 0.05$, typical in business research.

Step 3: State the critical values.

> The critical values are known to be at ± 1.96.

Step 4: Calculate the test statistic.

The Z-test statistic is computed using the following formula:

$$z = \frac{\overline{X} - \mu}{\frac{\sigma}{\sqrt{n}}}$$

where: $\overline{x}$ is the sample mean
μ is the population mean
σ is the population standard deviation
n is the sample size
the term $\frac{\sigma}{\sqrt{n}}$ is the standard error of the mean

Putting the data into the formula, we get

$$z = \frac{1.4 - 1.5}{\frac{0.15}{\sqrt{80}}} = -5.96$$

Step 5: Compare the test statistic value and the critical value.

The calculated value -5.96 is less than the lower critical value of -1.96.

Step 6: Come to a conclusion, either to reject H_0 or not.

Reject the Null hypothesis (H_0) at the 5% significance level.

Step 7: Put your conclusion into English.

The sample evidence does not support the store manager's claim that shoppers spend an average of $1.50 per week on jam and marmalade. The amount spent is significantly different from $1.50.

Example: Z-test for Two Independent Samples

In your MBA dissertation project, you wish to test the hypothesis that the proportion of engineers in a large firm who are exposed to a change-management program differs from the proportion of accounting personnel exposed to the change management program. Supposing 100 engineers and 100 accountants were sampled in the survey, and the proportion of engineers exposed to the change-management program was $p_1 = 0.35$ and that for accountants was $p_2 = 0.40$. Conduct the test at the 5% significance level.

Answer:

Step 1: State the hypothesis.

H_0 is such that the population proportion for the engineers is the same as that for the accountants.
H_1 is such that the population proportions are different.
In notation form (two-tail test):
$H_0: \pi_1 = \pi_2$
$H_1: \pi_1 \neq \pi_2$

Step 2: State the significance level.

Choose $\alpha = 0.05$, typical in business research.

Step 3: State the critical values.

The critical values are known to be at ± 1.96.

Step 4: Calculate the test statistic.

The Z-test statistic for differences of proportions is given by the following formula:

$$z = \frac{(p_1 - p_2) - (\pi_1 - \pi_2)}{S_{p_1 - p_2}}$$

where: p_1 = sample proportion of successes in group 1 (engineers)
p_2 = sample proportion of successes in group 2 (accountants)
π_1 = the population proportion of engineers
π_2 = the population proportion of the accountants
$S_{p_1-p_2}$ = the pooled estimate of the standard error of difference of proportions which can be computed using the following formula:

$$S_{p_1-p_2} = \sqrt{(\bar{p}\bar{q})\left(\frac{1}{n_1} + \frac{1}{n_2}\right)}$$

where: $\bar{p}$ = pooled estimate of proportion of successes in a sample of both groups
$\bar{q}$ = $(1-\bar{p})$ = pooled estimate of proportion of failures in a sample of both groups
n_1 = sample size for group 1
n_2 = sample size for group 2.

Since the population proportion π is unknown, we compute a weighted average of the sample proportion $\bar{p}$ using the following formula:

$$\bar{p} = \frac{n_1 p_1 + n_2 p_2}{n_1 + n_2}$$

$$= \frac{(100)(0.35)+(100)(0.40)}{100+100} = 0.375$$

The standard error of the difference of proportion is therefore computed as follows: $S_{p_1-p_2}$ = 0.068, and Z is computed as follows:

$$Z = \frac{(p_1-p_2)-(\pi_1-\pi_2)}{S_{p_1-p_2}} = \frac{(0.35-0.40)-(0)}{0.068} = -0.73$$

Step 5: Compare the test statistic value and the critical value.

The calculated value -0.73 is higher than the lower critical value of 1.96.

Step 6: Come to a conclusion, either to reject H_0 or not.

We cannot reject the Null hypothesis (H_0) at the 5% significance level.

Step 7: Put your conclusion into English.

There is no statistical difference in the proportion of engineers and in the proportion of accountants exposed to the change management program.

7.10.6 The Student t-Test of Hypothesis

The Student t-test (also known as the t-test) is used in research when the sample size is too small ($n \leq 30$) to be approximated by the standard normal distribution and when the population standard deviation σ is unknown. The t-distribution, just like the standard normal distribution, is a symmetrical, bell-shaped distribution with a mean of zero and a standard deviation of 1.

The t-distribution changes shape with the sample size changes, i.e., it is influenced by the number of degrees of freedom (v). The number of degrees of freedom is computed using the following formula:

$$v = n - 1$$

The t-test critical values for comparing with the test statistic value are read from statistical tables for a given level of significance and degrees of freedom.

Example: t-Test for One Sample

A lorry manufacturer claims the average annual maintenance cost for its vehicles is \$500. The maintenance department of one of their customers believes it to be higher and tests this by selecting a random sample of six lorries. The sample gives a mean annual maintenance cost of \$555 with a standard deviation of \$75.

Use an appropriate hypothesis test at the 5% significance level to see if the manufacturer's claim is true.

Answer:

Step 1: State the hypothesis.

H_0 is such that the population mean is \$500.
H_1 is such that the population mean is greater than \$500.
In notation form (one-tail test):
$H_0: \mu = \$500$
$H_1: \mu > \$500$

Note that the way one states the Null and Alternative hypotheses determines whether you have a one-tail or a two-tail test. This affects the choice of the critical value from the statistical table.

Step2: State the significance level.

Choose $\alpha = 0.05$, typical in business research.

Step 3: State the critical values.

The critical values are read from the t-tables (see Appendix 4) at $v = n - 1 = 6 - 1 = 5$ degrees of freedom, and at 5% significance level.

The t-critical value $t_{\alpha,v} = 2.015$.

Step 4: Calculate the test statistic.

The t-test statistic is computed using the following formula:

$$t = \frac{\overline{X} - \mu}{\frac{S}{\sqrt{n}}}$$

where: $\overline{X}$ is the sample mean
μ is the population mean
S is the sample standard deviation
n is the sample size
the term $\frac{S}{\sqrt{n}}$ is the standard error of the mean

Putting the data into the formula, we get:

$$t = \frac{555 - 500}{\frac{75}{\sqrt{6}}} = 1.796$$

Step 5: Compare the test statistic value and the critical value.

The calculated value 1.796 is lower than the critical value of 2.015.

Step 6: Come to a conclusion, either to reject H_0 or not.

We cannot reject the Null hypothesis (H_0) at the 5% significance level.

Step 7: Put your conclusion into English.

The sample evidence does not show that the average annual maintenance is more than $500.

Example: t-Test for Two Independent Samples or Groups

A researcher wants to test the difference between male and female ESAMI MBA students in scores on an interval scale measuring attitude toward business. A high score on the scale meant a favourable attitude toward business. In the study, 21 female students and 14 male students were sampled. The mean score for female students was 16.5 with a standard deviation of 2.1, whereas the mean score for male students was 12.2 with a standard deviation of 2.6. Conduct the test at 5% level of significance.

Answer:

Step 1: State the hypothesis.

H$_0$ is such that there is no difference in attitudes (mean scores) toward business.
H$_1$ is such that there is a difference in attitudes (mean scores) toward business.
In notation form (two-tail test):
H$_0$: $\mu_1 = \mu_2$
H1: $\mu_1 \neq \mu_2$.

Step2: State the significance level.

Choose $\alpha = 0.05$, typical in business research.

Step 3: State the critical values.

The critical values are read from the t-tables (see Appendix 4) at $v = n - k$, where $n = n_1 + n_2 = 21 + 14 = 35$, and k = number of groups = 2. The number of degrees of freedom is therefore $v = 35 - 2 = 33$. At 5% significance level, the t-critical value $t_{\alpha,v} = 2.042$.

Step 4: Calculate the test statistic.

The t-test statistic is computed using the following formula:

$$t = \frac{\bar{x}_1 - \bar{x}_2}{S_{\bar{x}_1-\bar{x}_2}}$$

where

$$S_{\bar{x}_1-\bar{x}_2} = \sqrt{\left(\frac{(n_1-1)\left(S_1^2\right)+ (n_2-1)\left(S_2^2\right)}{n_1+n_2-2}\right)\left(\frac{1}{n_1} + \frac{1}{n_2}\right)} = 0.797$$

is the pooled standard error of the difference between means of independent samples.

The t-test statistic is therefore computed to be

$$t = \frac{\bar{x}_1-\bar{x}_2}{S_{\bar{x}_1-\bar{x}_2}} = \frac{16.5-12.2}{0.797} = \frac{4.3}{0.797} = 5.395$$

Step 5: Compare the test statistic value and the critical value.

The calculated value 5.395 is much higher than the critical value of 2.042.

Step 6: Come to a conclusion, either to reject H_0 or not.

We reject the Null hypothesis (H_0) at the 5% significance level.

Step 7: Put your conclusion into English.

The sample evidence does show that there is a difference in attitudes (mean scores) toward business. The results show that the female students' attitude scores are significantly higher than those of male students.

7.10.7 The χ^2—Test of Hypothesis

The *Chi-squared* (χ^2) test is a non-parametric test which is used to assess the statistical significance of a finding by testing for contingency (uncertainty of occurrence) or goodness of fit. The test allows us to test for significance in the analysis of frequency distributions. Thus *nominal* categorical data on variables such as gender, education, or dichotomous responses may be analysed statistically.

The standard seven steps of hypothesis testing are as follows for the χ^2 test:

Step 1: State the hypothesis to be tested. The Null hypothesis is always assumed to be true.

Step2: State the significance level. Typically for business research, a 5% or 1% level of significance is commonly used.

Step 3: State the critical values.

Just like the t-distribution, the χ^2 distribution is not just a single probability curve but a family of curves. These curves vary in shape with the sample size (*n*) or degrees of freedom (*v*). The number of degrees of freedom is computed using the following formula:

For a one-way frequency data table, $v = n - 1$.

For an *n*-way frequency data table, $v = (r - 1)(c - 1)$, where *r* is the number of rows and *c* is the number of columns in the frequency data table.

The critical value of the χ^2 test is $\chi^2_{\alpha,v}$ which is read from the χ^2 statistical tables at a given level of significance (α) and number of degrees of freedom (v) .

Step 4: Calculate the test statistic.

The χ^2 test statistic is computed using the following formula:

$$\chi2 = \sum_i \frac{(O_i - E_i)^2}{E_i}$$

where: O_i = observed frequency in the i-th cell
         E_i = expected frequency in the i-th cell

For each cell, the expected frequency is computed using the following formula:

$$E_I = \frac{Row\ total\ X\ Column\ total}{Grand\ total}$$

Step 5: Compare the test statistic value and the critical value.

Step 6: Come to a conclusion, either to reject H_0 or not.

Step 7: Put your conclusion into English.

Example: χ^2—Test of Hypothesis

The purchase of different beer brands (with different alcoholic strengths) is thought to be associated with the gender of the drinker.

A brewery has commissioned a survey to find if this is true with the following results:

Gender of Drinker	Strength of Beer		
	High	Medium	Low
Male	20	50	30
Female	10	55	35

Answer:

Step 1: State the hypothesis.

H_0: There is no association between gender and strength of beer.
H_1: There is an association between gender & strength of beer.

Step2: State the significance level.

Choose α = 0.05, typical in business research.

Step 3: State the critical values.

The number of degrees of freedom is $v = (r - 1)(c - 1) = (2 - 1)$
$(3 - 1) = 2$.
The critical value is read from the χ^2-tables (see Appendix 5), and
is as follows: $\chi^2_{\alpha,v} \chi^2_{\alpha,v} = 5.99$.

Step 4: Calculate the test statistic.

First, we prepare a contingency table with row totals, column totals,
and grand total as follows:

	Strength of Beer			Row Total
Gender	High	Medium	Low	
Male	20	50	30	100
Female	10	55	35	100
Column Total	30	105	65	200

The χ^2 test statistic is computed using the following formula:

$$\chi 2 = \sum_i \frac{(O_i - E_i)^2}{E_i}$$

Using the contingency table, the expected values are computed are summarised in the table below:

O_i	E_i	(O_i-E_i)	$(O_i-E_i)^2$	$(O_i-E_i)^2/E_i$
20	15	5	25	1.667
10	15	-5	25	1.667
50	52.5	-2.5	6.25	0.119
55	52.5	2.5	6.25	0.119
30	32.5	-2.5	6.25	0.192
35	32.5	2.5	6.25	0.192
		$\chi^2=$		3.956

Step 5: Compare the test statistic value and the critical value.

The Chi-test statistic value 3.956 is clearly less than the critical value 5.99.

Step 6: Come to a conclusion, either to reject H_0 or not.

We cannot reject the Null hypothesis.

Step 7: Put your conclusion into English.

There appears to be no association between the gender of the drinker and the strength of beer at the 5% level of significance.

Note that when there is a small number of counts in the contingency table, the use of the chi-square test statistic may not be appropriate. Specifically, is recommended that this test not be used if any cell in the table has an expected value of less than one, or if eighty per cent of the cells have an expected value that is less than five. Under this scenario, the *Fisher's exact test* is recommended for conducting tests of hypothesis.

CHAPTER EIGHT

WRITING THE RESEARCH REPORT

8.1 INTRODUCTION

Which report should you write?

There are two reports that you can write.
- the report you had in mind when you designed your study
- the report that makes sense after you have seen the results

Figure 8.1 The Research Process

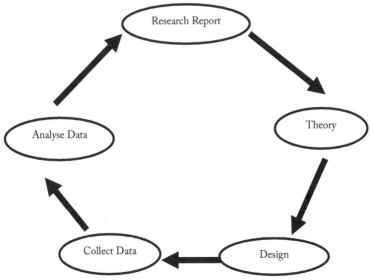

Your overriding purpose should be to tell the world what you have learned from your study. You should use an "hourglass" form in your the report.

Start broad and present the general structure. Then get "narrow" and give the specifics of your study. End by broadening out again to more general considerations.

What is the problem being investigated?

1. Your first task is to introduce the background.
2. Describe the nature of the problem being investigated.
3. Place the questions and issues into a larger context so that we know the general significance. Confirm to the "hourglass" shape.
4. Write in English prose, not jargon.
5. Lead the reader up to the formal or theoretical statement.

8.1.1 The Literature Review

1. Summarise the current state of knowledge in the area of investigation.
2. What previous research has been done on this problem?
3. What pertinent theories of the phenomenon are there, if any?
4. Familiarise yourself with previous work on the topic before you design your own study.
5. It will assist you if you record your study of the literature.

You can also use a slight different approach:

1. Cite references you had not previously consulted.
2. Cite only articles pertinent to the specific issues with which you are dealing.

3. Emphasise their major conclusions, findings, or relevant methodological issues.
4. Books and articles are cited in the text of the report, giving the author's last name and date of publication, e.g., "According to Mwape (1972), people find research difficult. Not everyone agrees with this conclusion, for example Mumba (1980)."

As you come to the end of the introduction, introduce your own study in brief overview, e.g., "The question then is whether or not such practices discourage research. The present study sought to answer this question by . . ."

8.1.2   Method

What should you include?

The reader needs to know how the study was carried out. What was its basic design? If the study was experimental, just what were the experimental manipulations?

If data was collected, what means were used, e.g., questionnaire, interview etc.?

What questions were asked?

1. The reader needs to know how observations for replies to questions were translated into measures of variables.
2. The reader needs to be told the sample size.
3. Who were the subjects?
4. How many were there?
5. How were they selected?

These questions are useful to estimate a generalization of your findings.

8.1.3   Result and Discussions

You should use the following approach to presenting your results.

1.   Results are discussed as they are presented.
2.   This section ends with two or three paragraphs that state the conclusions reached.
3.   You should mention any qualifications imposed by problems encountered in executing and analysing the study.
4.   You should suggest what further research might be appropriate.

You set the stage before presenting the main results. In the preliminary matter you need to present evidence that your study successfully set up the conclusions for testing your hypothesis or answering your questions.

When presenting the findings, start with your central findings, and then elaborate or qualify it as necessary.

All books and articles cited in the text of the research are listed at the end alphabetically in the References section.

In the Summary or Abstract, you should outline the problem, your procedures, your major findings, and the major conclusion drawn from them, along with your recommendations.

8.1.4   Validity and Reliability in Research Design

Research is *valid* when its conclusions are true. It is *reliable* when its findings are repeatable. Validity and reliability are requirements for both the design and measure of research. At the level of research development we examine the conclusions and ask whether they are true and repeatable.

There are three types of validity.

1. A thesis has internal validity when research accounting identifies causal relationships. Internal validity requires that you are able to rule out rival explanations to demonstrate that your conclusion is valid.
2. Research has *construct validity* when it properly identifies or "names" the variables under study.
3. Research has external validity when the findings obtained on a small sample apply to the whole target population.

Reliable research findings are repeatable. The conclusion can be generalized beyond the particular conditions of the initial research. It can be repeated or replicated.

Theories are a large body of interconnected propositions about how social work operates. *Hypotheses* are a smaller body of propositions derived from theories and developed into theories.

8.1.5   Summary, Conclusions, and Recommendations

A summary of key findings from the data should be prepared. Conclusions should be drawn from the findings and practical recommendations made to solve the problem being investigated.

8.2   DETAILED THESIS STRUCTURE

A typical thesis should be structured as follows:

COVER PAGE
COPYRIGHT STATEMENT
DECLARATION STATEMENT
ACKNOWLEDGEMENTS
ABSTRACT

LIST OF FIGURES, TABLES, ABBREVIATIONS, AND ACRONYMS
TABLE OF CONTENTS
CHAPTER 1: INTRODUCTION
CHAPTER 2: LITERATURE REVIEW
CHAPTER 3: THEORETICAL FRAMEWORK
CHAPTER 4: METHODOLOGY
CHAPTER 5: DATA ANLYSIS, FINDINGS, AND DISCUSSION
CHAPTER 6: CONCLUSION
REFERENCE LIST
APPENDICES

8.2.1 The Cover Page

The cover page of your thesis must be structured as shown in Appendix 3. It should be noted that there may be slight variations in the wording. However, the key elements on the cover page should be your thesis title, your name, the type of degree awarded, the name of the awarding institution, and the date you submitted your thesis.

A thesis title must be concise and brief, without unnecessary articles and repeated words. For example, consider the following title:

A Study of Factors Causing Poverty in Malawi: A Case of Mzimba District, Mzimba, Malawi

This title could be shortened as follows:

Factors Causing Poverty in Malawi: A Case of Mzimba District

8.2.2 The Copyright Statement

You may wish to write a copyright statement in your thesis to show that this is your work and that anyone using your work must duly acknowledge. The copyright statement makes your work appear formal. The copyright can be in your own name, but it is courteous of you to give dual ownership of your work to yourself and to the school. A copyright statement might look like this:

> Copyright © Eastern and Southern African Management Institute, 2009.
>
> All rights reserved. The copyright of this thesis belongs to the author under the MBA thesis regulations of the Eastern and Southern African Management Institute. Due acknowledgement must be given at all times when using material taken from this thesis. Permission to reproduce any part of this thesis must be obtained from the author or from the Eastern and Southern African Management Institute.

8.2.3 The Declaration Statement

The declaration of authorship is a formal certification of authorship. In this section, you need to confirm that this is indeed your own work and that where other people's ideas have been used, you have dully acknowledged. You are also confirming that this work has only been submitted for this particular MBA award offered by your school, and not submitted for another award to a different school. Appendix 7 shows a sample of the declaration statement.

8.2.4 The Acknowledgement Statement

The acknowledgement section is placed at the beginning of your thesis and not at the end. In this section you acknowledge the help and support various people rendered to you during your study. These people may include your supervisor, faculty members, family members, sources of your data, or bosses and colleagues at your workplace.

8.2.5   The Abstract

The abstract gives a synopsis of your thesis. It is the equivalent of the executive summary in reports. The abstract will be the first part of your thesis that will be read by people, and as such it should be written in a professional and concise manner. The language to be used here should be clear and to the point. The abstract should include paragraphs on the following issues and questions:

1. Introduction
2. What was the research problem you investigated? What was the purpose of your research? What were your research objectives?
3. What was your research methodology?
4. What were your main findings?
5. What is the meaning and implication of your findings, that is, what were your conclusions and recommendations?

The abstract should not just be a cut-and-paste of some chapter(s). It should be written in your original language. The abstract should not be too long. One single page is adequate for the abstract. It should be noted that the abstract is the last part of your thesis that you will write. For a sample abstract, see Appendixes 8 and 9 (Sample MBA Theses).

8.2.6   The List of Figures, Tables, Abbreviations, and Acronyms

You may wish to include a list of figures and tables in your thesis. If the lists are too large and make your thesis look too big, then you may wish to leave them out. The lists do help the reader to make sense of your thesis and enable him or her to locate them easily inside your thesis (since lists show page numbers). See the following sample Lists of Figures and Tables:

LIST OF FIGURES

LIST OF TABLES

If you are fond of using acronyms and abbreviations, these should be explained in this part of your thesis. See the following example:

LIST OF ACRONYMS

NPO   — Non-Profit Organizations/Not-for-Profit Organizations
FPO   — For-Profit Organizations
NGO   — Non-Governmental Organizations
INGO   — International Non-Governmental Organizations
LNGO — Local Non-Governmental Organizations
VCO   — Voluntary and Charitable Organizations
CSO   — Civil-Society Organizations
CBO   — Community-Based Organizations
FBO   — Faith-Based Organizations
ABB   — Activity-Based Budgeting
ZBB   — Zero-Based Budgeting
PPBS   — Program Planning and Budgeting Systems
IB   — Incremental Budgeting
ICPAK — Institute of Certified Public Accountants of Kenya
GAAP — Generally Accepted Accounting Principles

8.2.7   The Table of Contents

You should prepare a table of contents which will help the reader to see how your thesis is structured. This implies that the hierarchy of chapters, sections, and subsections and the corresponding page numbers should match those in the body of your thesis. The table of contents is one of the last sections that you write in your thesis.

See Appendixes 8 and 9 for examples of the Table of Contents.

8.2.8   The Introduction Chapter

In the introduction chapter, you introduce the reader to the research problem you investigated and the reasons why it is important to investigate the problem.

For the *quantitative research approach* (see Appendix 8 for a sample thesis using this approach), the following structure is appropriate for the introduction chapter:

CHAPTER 1:   INTRODUCTION

1.1   Overview (*Introduce the problem and its context, about two pages.*)

1.2   Problem Definition (*about one paragraph*)

1.3   Research Objective (*about one paragraph*)

1.4   Theoretical Framework (*Give a brief summary of your theoretical framework; details should be given in the theoretical framework chapter.*)

    1.4.1   Dependent Variables (*brief definition*)

    1.4.2   Independent Variables (*brief definition*)

    1.4.3   Moderating Variables (*brief definition*)

    1.4.4   Intervening Variables (*brief definition*)

    1.4.5   Assumptions (*List the key assumptions.*)

    1.4.6   Limitations (*List the key limitations.*)

1.5   Research Questions and Hypotheses

    1.5.1   Major Research Questions (*This is the general focus research question reflecting your research topic.*)

    1.5.2   Minor Research Questions (*List them and introduce them briefly.*)

    1.5.3   Research Hypotheses (*State them. They should be projected answers to the research questions.*)

1.6   Thesis Structure

For a *qualitative research approach* (see Appendix 9 for a sample thesis using this approach) the following structure for the introduction chapter should be used:

CHAPTER 1: INTRODUCTION

1.1 Overview
1.2 Problem Definition
1.3 Research Objective
1.4 Theoretical Framework
    1.4.1 Research Variables
    1.4.2 Assumptions
    1.4.3 Limitations
1.5 Research Questions and Propositions
    1.5.1 Major Research Questions
    1.5.2 Minor Research Questions
    1.5.3 Research Propositions
1.6 Thesis Structure

Another variation of the structure of the introduction chapter is follows:

CHAPTER 1: INTRODUCTION

1.1 Background
1.2 Problem Statement
1.3 Research Questions
1.4 Research Objectives (or Purpose)
1.5 Research Hypotheses (or Propositions)
1.6 Delineation and Limitations
1.7 Definition of Terms and Concepts
1.8 Assumptions
1.9 Significance of the Study
1.10 Brief Chapter Overview

The introduction chapter should be about 6-10 pages long.

8.2.9   The Literature Review Chapter

The literature review provides your thesis with a solid grounding. It is the backbone of your thesis. The literature review should be written in a comprehensive and critical manner, contextualizing it all to your current research study. This means that it should contain a detailed theory base relating to your work, a survey of best practices and ideas in the world, and the survey of past research relating to your work.

Hofstee (2006), cites the following purposes of the literature review:

1.   It makes you aware of what is going on in the field, and thus gives you your credentials.
2.   It shows that there is a theory base for the study you are proposing.
3.   It provides a detailed context for your work by showing what has been done before.
4.   It shows that your work has significance.
5.   It shows that your work leads to new knowledge.

Structure your literature review chapter to include the following:

1.   A historical overview of how the topic or subject has been previously researched. You can write this in a chronological order. You should show the progression of past works and how it leads to your research topic.
2.   A description of the most relevant theories and models that have been used in similar studies in the past.
3.   Past researchers who have worked in similar studies. Their findings should be discussed and linked to your current study. Group the works by topic, idea, or research question. Identify gaps in past research and make a case for your current study. This is what would make your work look original.

This chapter should be about 20-22 pages long.

8.2.10 The Theoretical Framework Chapter

Write your theoretical framework to include the following:

1. Identify and label the variables which can help explain the dynamics and context of your research problem.
2. State the relationships among the variables of interest to the research problem.
3. Theorize the nature and direction of the relationships. Are these relationships your own, or are they based on some existing theory or model? The existing theory or model must be given with proper citation of the source.
4. Citing the relevant literature, explain logically how or why these relationships should exist. What possible effects might emerge from these relationships?
5. Construct a conceptual model or schematic diagram to show how the variables are related.

8.2.11 The Methodology Chapter

Figure 8.2 shows the generic structure of the method chapter.

Figure 8.2 Structure of the Methodology Chapter

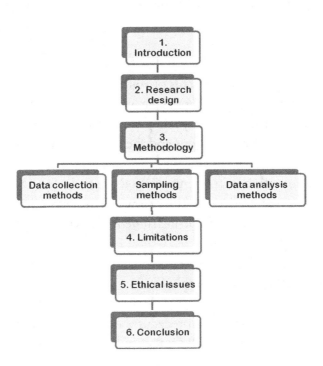

Introduction

Start the method chapter with an introduction section where you restate the research problem statement and purpose of the study, you outline the results the method was designed to generate, and you give an overview of the chapter.

Research Design

Start this section by giving a narration of your research paradigm. Are you a positivist or a phenomenologist or somewhere in between? Are you using a deductive or inductive approach in your research? Discuss the research designs (that is, types or techniques) you used to answer your research questions. What are the strengths and weaknesses of these techniques? Support your discussion with relevant literature.

Data Collection Methods

In this section you provide details of your data collection methods and sources of data. You explain how your variables were measured. Data can be collected from secondary and primary sources depending on the nature of your research questions and the variables involved.

What data collection instruments did you use and why? Did you use a questionnaire or interview checklist? How was the instrument designed? What was the purpose of the instrument? Discuss the validity and reliability of the instrument.

Sampling Methods And Sample Size

What sampling methods and procedures did you use and why? Was a sampling frame readily available for the study, and can you show it? What was the sample size used in the study, and how was it determined?

Characterize your study population. What sampling design did you use—probability or non-probability sampling? What sampling procedure did you use, and why? What was your sample size, and how was it determined?

Data Analysis Methods

What data analysis methods did you use, and why? Did you use statistical tests of hypothesis, or did you use a computer package such as SPSS? What computations did the statistical package actually do?

Limitations

Discuss any methodological limitations you experienced in your study.

Ethical Issues

Discuss any ethical issues that you encountered in your research. What measures did you use to mitigate those factors?

Conclusion

Round off the chapter with a one paragraph section of how this chapter was structured.

8.2.12 The Data Analysis, Findings, and Discussion Chapter

Descriptive Data Analysis

Start this section by describing the data you collected. Report on the results of your test for goodness of data, e.g., the Cronbach Alpha.

Present your descriptive statistics relating to each research question or proposition. These can be in the form of pie charts, bar graphs, frequency distributions, and tables. The results of hypothesis tests or answering research questions should be presented in the next section, unless your research used the case study approach, in which case you cannot generalize your results to the entire population.

Inferential Data Analysis

Inferential statistical results are used if you want to generalize your sample results to the entire population. State the statistical tests you performed, including the significance levels that you used. State whether the results are leading to rejecting or accepting your research hypothesis and whether they are answering the research question or not.

Findings and Discussion

Findings can take many forms, ranging from responses to your questionnaire, data from secondary sources, or results from an experiment.

Analyse and discuss the findings with the aim of coming to a conclusion on your hypotheses or research questions.

Each finding should be analysed and discussed in order to come to a sub-conclusion. Each sub-conclusion will contribute to the final conclusion as to whether the hypothesis or research question has been substantiated or not. Analysis and discussion of each finding should be based on past research work and the literature presented in your literature review.

8.2.13 The Conclusion Chapter

The conclusion chapter is the last chapter of your thesis. Most students entitle this chapter, "Summary of Key Findings, Conclusions, and Recommendations". This chapter should be structured with the following sections:

1. Introduction
2. Summary of findings
3. Conclusions
4. Summary of contributions
5. Recommendations

Introduction

Start the conclusion chapter by reminding the reader what your research problem is and what your research objective is as stated in Chapter One. You should also briefly present your theoretical model, research techniques, and the methodologies that you used in your study. All this should be put in single paragraph.

Summary of Findings

Recap your main findings and sub-conclusions from the previous chapter in order to prime the reader for the coming conclusions. Do not present new results or data in this chapter.

Conclusions

Conclusions are deductions from your research study. Conclusions state whether your hypothesis is true or false, they state whether your research question has been answered or not. The conclusions should relate back to the research hypotheses and/or research questions. In the absence of research hypotheses and research questions, at the minimum your conclusions should relate back to your problem statement or your research objectives. Do not present new data here.

Summary Of Contributions

In this section, present the significance of your conclusions. In what way have your study and conclusions generated new knowledge in this field of study? Discuss the implications of this new knowledge.

Also discuss any theoretical and practical implications of your study. For example, does your work change any past paradigm or not? If so, state how. Show how these relate broadly to the significance section or research objectives presented in Chapter One.

Recommendations

Present your recommendations for applying your research results. Recommendations can also be your proposed solutions to solve the problem you investigated. Recommendations must be feasible and practical to implement. They must be based on the key findings of your study. Recommendations should not come from outside your work based on your own excitement or wishful thinking.

Include in this section recommendations for further research in order to guide future researchers to answer new questions that your study might have raised or to apply your study's approach in different contexts. This provides continuity in the process of generating knowledge.

8.2.14 The References or Endnotes List

List all the references cited in your thesis in alphabetical order or numerical order for endnotes. Use the Turabian system to list your references (Turabian, 1996).

8.2.15 The Appendices

Appendices include materials that support or substantiate points made in the body of your thesis. Appendices include things that can disrupt you thesis flow if they were put in the body of the thesis, either because they are somewhat bulky or because they are not directly linked to your research hypotheses or research questions.

Appendices can include a copy of your blank questionnaire, interview checklist, and other bulky materials.

Appendices should be listed in your table of contents, and they should be cited accordingly in the thesis.

REFERENCES

Campbell, D., and Fiske, D. (1959). "Convergence and Discriminant Validation by Multitrait-Multimethod Matrix," In *Psychological Bulletin*, 56, pp. 81-105.

Campbell. D., and Stanley, J. (1963). *Experimental and Quasi-Experimental Designs for Research*, Belmont: Wadsworth Publishing.

Collis, J., and Hussey, R. (2003). Business Research: A Practical Guide for Undergraduate and Postgraduate Students, Hampshire, UK: Palgrave MacMillan.

Cronbach, L. J. (1951). "Coefficient Alpha and the Internal Structure of Tests," *Psychometrika, 16(3)*, 297-334. deVaus, D.A. (1991). *Surveys in Social Research*, London: UCL Press and Allen & Unwin. deVaus, D.A. (1996). *Surveys in Social Research* (4th edition), London: UCL Press.

Dillman, D.A. (1978). Mail and Telephone Surveys: the Total Design Method, New York: John Wiley.

Dunn, W. (1981). *Public Policy Analysis: An Introduction*. Englewood Cliffs, NJ: Prentice Hall.

Francis, A. (2004). *Business Mathematics and Statistics* (6th edition), London: Thomson Learning.

Gill, J., and Johnson, P. (1991). *Research Methods for Managers*, London: Paul Chapman Publishing.

Healey, M.J. (1991). "Obtaining Information from Businesses," in Healey, M.J. (ed.), *Economic Activity and Land Use: the Changing Information Base for Local and Regional Studies*, Harlow: Longman, pp. 193-250.

Henry, G.T. (1990). *Practical Sampling*, Newbury Park, CA, U.S.A.: Sage.

Hofstee, E. (2006). *Constructing a Good Dissertation*, Johannesburg: EPE Publishing.

Howard, K., and Sharp, J.A. (1983). *The Management of a Student Research Project*, Aldershot: Gower.

Hussey, J., and Hussey, R. (1997). *Business Research: A Practical Guide for Undergraduate and Postgraduate Students*, London: MacMillan.

Kervin, J.B. (1992). *Methods for Business Research*, New York: HarperCollins.

Leedy, P.D. (1997). *Practical Research Planning and Design*, Columbus Ohio, U.S.A.: Merrill (Imprint of Prentice Hall).

Lynn, P., Beerten, R., Laiho, J., and Martin, J. (2001). "Recommended Standard Final Outcome Categories and Standard Definitions of Response Rate for Social Surveys", *Working Papers of the Institute for Social and Economic Research*, paper 2001-23. Colchester, UK: University of Essex.

Mugenda, O.M., and Mugenda, A.G. (1999). *Research Methods: Quantitative and Qualitative Approaches*, Nairobi, Acts Press.

Owen, F., and Jones, R. (1994). *Statistics* (4th edn), London: Pitman Publishing.

Nachmias, D., and Nachmias, C. (1976). *Research Methods in Social Sciences*, New York: St. Martin's Press.

Nachmias, D., and Nachmias, C. (1981). *Research Methods in Social Sciences*, New York: St. Martin's Press.

Robson, C. (2002). Real World Research: A Resource for Social Scientists and Practitioner Researchers, New Jersey: Wiley Blackwell.

Saunders, M., Lewis, P., and Thornhill, A. (2007). *Research Methods for Business Students*, Harlow, UK: Pearson Education.

Sekaran, U. (2003). Research Methods for Business: A Skill Building Approach, New York: John Wiley.

Shajahan, S. (2005). *Research Methods for Management*, Mumbai: Jaico Publishing.

Simon, J.L. (1978). *Basic Research Methods in Social Science*, New York: Random House.

Stat Trek (2007). *Random Number Generator*, (Internet), Available at: http://stattrek.com. Accessed on 4 February 2009.

The Zimbabwe Society of Health, (2002). *Simplified Research Methods Series I, II, III*, Harare: The Zimbabwe Society of Health.

Turabian, K.L. (1996) *A Manual for Writers of Term Papers, Theses and Dissertations*, 6th Edition, Chicago: University of Chicago Press.

Zikmund, W.G. (2003). *Business Research Methods*, Mason, Ohio: South Western.

A Sample of ESAMI Executive MBA Student Dissertation Titles

1. Impact of business development services on the business development of micro, small, and medium enterprises sector in Malawi: A diagnostic study
2. The influence of workplace trust over performance of public health workers in Tanzania
3. Factors that affect compliance with the new national procurement policy and procedures in Zambia
4. Do the existing Kenyan pension schemes adequately cater for the needs of retirees? A case study of Mombasa and Embu retirees
5. The impact of customer care oriented culture on service delivery. A case study of Zimbabwe utility companies
6. The state of corporate environmental reporting in Kenya
7. Environmental health management of solid medical waste disposal: A case study of Bugando Medical Centre in Mwanza, Tanzania
8. Gender aspects of HIV/AIDS: Addressing the vulnerability of women and girls
9. Analysing alternative sources of funding for higher education in Malawi
10. Accessibility to medication for opportunistic infections by people living with HIV/AIDS: The case of Arusha Municipality, Tanzania

11. Early death after retirement: Case study of social security institutions in Tanzania
12. The roles of commercial banks in facilitating international trade: The case of Tanzania
13. The paradox of privatization: Case of Tanzania Telecommunications Company Limited
14. Assessing the progress in effectiveness of financial management systems of local community based organizations: A case study of RTI-WAPP grantees in Uganda
15. The impact of liberalization and independent regulation on the electricity sector: The Uganda case
16. Analysis of factors affecting the competitiveness of the cement industry in Tanzania
17. The causes of the decline in Zimbabwe's economic performance and the role of monetary policy in turning around an economy under stress in an unstable political environment
18. Training and its impact on the performance of small and medium enterprises in Kampala
19. Budget management through tracking and monitoring in international non-governmental organizations in Kenya
20. Dimensions in the development of Kenya Government bond index
21. Factors affecting succession planning in businesses owned by the Agikuyu in Kenya
22. An evaluation of human resource systems and practices in financial institutions: The case of banks in Lusaka, Zambia
23. The impact of non-traditional exports on employment, foreign exchange earnings, and personal incomes in Africa: The case of vanilla in Uganda
24. The direct economic impact of the operations of the United Nations International Criminal Tribunal for Rwanda on Arusha
25. The applicability of corporate governance principles in statutory corporations in Malawi

26. Implications of the demand-driven approach on accessibility to rural safe water in Uganda: A case study of selected districts
27. Factors influencing expiry of drugs in a military pharmaceutical department
28. Implications of dual membership to SADC and COMESA on Malawi's trade
29. The effect of poor natural resources management on women in Zimbabwean rural communities
30. Organizational transformation and its impact on customer satisfaction: The case of National Water and Sewerage Corporation in Uganda
31. The management of used oil in Tanzania
32. An analysis of pesticides trading practices: A case study of the role of SATEC trading practices on pesticides impact on the environment in Tanzania
33. The impact of mobile phone telecommunications development on the environment: The case study of Dar es Salaam, Tanzania
34. A survey of automotive fuel adulteration practices in Kenya

APPENDIX 2

Random Sampling Numbers

86 30 31 80 11 07 09 19 73 98 53 78 33 69 46 15 42 32 32 74 01 26 70
78 95 79 21 35 33 92 12 38 06 92 14 39 49 19 21 72 77 49 38 12 35 96
24 70 28 77 17 86 21 28 59 54 02 85 35 54 41 55 66 23 60 20 67 45 73
09 45 68 62 71 09 55 61 77 86 61 26 34 26 99 66 16 90 26 80 66 34 39
15 35 28 71 14 02 35 02 21 48 80 52 80 97 85 26 31 52 72 94 34 78 03
21 87 05 40 47 35 43 23 74 53 28 94 87 19 81 91 96 73 41 29 81 57 25
57 11 77 04 48 61 83 80 65 61 40 74 35 79 15 89 52 83 83 56 85 62 24
63 48 56 50 25 45 95 70 70 02 93 29 76 12 66 16 02 46 33 06 98 90 20
83 12 79 15 15 93 37 47 93 00 28 21 51 91 07 19 98 19 25 86 37 35 95
04 08 62 51 51 96 04 09 79 80 03 50 46 32 81 83 13 61 02 07 87 13 05
43 38 85 75 76 82 56 53 66 71 98 35 95 45 58 45 33 11 15 94 33 14 65
41 17 17 59 40 59 09 24 46 80 31 35 62 93 52 74 95 55 03 93 27 51 22
96 78 00 40 35 77 98 66 23 59 71 79 62 56 58 24 50 39 31 37 97 47 79
02 36 80 19 65 94 27 40 76 39 73 00 71 73 74 88 54 68 76 54 80 48 65
11 89 11 57 75 53 64 39 96 18 89 30 22 12 32 23 90 90 32 36 78 03 63
35 37 51 34 57 35 15 52 53 04 27 28 15 24 76 99 93 70 24 30 76 29 46
30 49 72 85 44 56 20 21 83 27 30 49 69 50 99 40 62 43 70 11 68 19 66
12 14 65 44 51 62 33 40 07 01 44 85 24 73 57 48 95 03 95 70 99 54 39
02 34 45 73 57 46 05 85 30 61 91 93 60 50 66 58 53 55 00 18 41 61 70
72 30 96 66 69 86 44 68 59 93 13 32 23 27 77 80 48 88 40 23 86 28 40
44 48 52 06 33 18 88 78 17 08 06 48 86 75 13 35 42 69 24 18 44 80 07
64 04 37 13 28 38 80 33 20 53 89 69 94 57 20 55 04 47 42 37 34 85 57
71 52 23 10 85 55 51 15 56 44 46 42 47 08 68 37 21 37 11 04 17 61 68
57 73 76 44 25 71 50 59 99 17 21 09 45 96 19 11 66 47 69 98 37 87 06

14 17 95 92 84 37 20 32 27 67 51 39 92 30 20 68 61 57 24 84 09 99 72
02 76 31 76 04 60 49 10 32 33 15 18 91 98 58 55 19 11 70 27 37 66 90
43 87 66 79 14 74 86 22 92 78 96 21 75 60 52 89 75 88 72 28 73 45 54
96 68 93 03 04 13 32 68 80 09 80 65 20 59 33 48 18 97 46 17 47 10 43
21 56 03 33 88 87 81 02 70 83 14 53 25 20 53 44 12 78 30 11 04 58 30
74 44 40 43 38 88 01 19 96 77 12 69 17 59 03 67 49 19 55 63 53 24 64
02 17 76 40 45 03 99 53 05 68 93 62 10 96 42 88 25 11 25 34 11 74 11
84 89 26 10 15 60 24 14 15 80 35 80 63 46 71 18 13 40 32 00 06 44 61
55 04 43 62 70 62 57 09 26 99 11 77 31 21 77 20 83 69 34 91 06 29 44
14 42 41 63 90 13 02 38 78 28 37 15 48 75 47 04 39 33 65 05 46 76 12
24 69 86 44 68 59 93 13 32 23

Source: Stat Trek (2007).

APPENDIX 3

Critical Values for
Pearson's Correlation Coefficient, r

Critical Values for Pearson's Correlation Coefficient, r

(= N - 2) (N = number of pairs)	Level of Significance for One-Tailed Test			
	.05	.025	.01	.005
	Level of Significance for Two-Tailed Test			
	.10	.05	.02	.01
1	.988	.997	.9995	.9999
2	.900	.950	.980	.990
3	.805	.878	.934	.959
4	.729	.811	.882	.917
5	.669	.754	.833	.874
6	.622	.707	.789	.834
7	.582	.666	.750	.798
8	.549	.632	.716	.765
9	.521	.602	.685	.735
10	.497	.576	.658	.708
11	.476	.553	.634	.684
12	.458	.532	.612	.661
13	.441	.514	.592	.641
14	.426	.497	.574	.628
15	.412	.482	.558	.606

16	.400	.468	.542	.590
17	.389	.456	.528	.575
18	.378	.444	.516	.561
19	.369	.433	.503	.549
20	.360	.423	.492	.537
21	.352	.413	.482	.526
22	.344	.404	.472	.515
23	.337	.396	.462	.505
24	.330	.388	.453	.495
25	.323	.381	.445	.487
26	.317	.374	.437	.479
27	.311	.367	.430	.471
28	.306	.361	.423	.463
29	.301	.355	.416	.456
30	.296	.349	.409	.449
35	.275	.325	.381	.418
40	.257	.304	.358	.393
45	.243	.288	.338	.372
50	.231	.273	.322	.354
60	.211	.250	.295	.325
70	.195	.232	.274	.302
80	.183	.217	.256	.284
90	.173	.205	.242	.267
100	.164	.195	.230	.254

Source: Stat Trek (2007).

APPENDIX 4

The t Distribution Critical Values

	Proportion in One Tail					
	0.25	0.10	0.05	0.025	0.01	0.005
	Proportion in Two Tails					
Df	0.50	0.20	0.10	0.05	0.02	0.01
1	1.000	3.078	6.314	12.706	31.821	63.657
2	0.816	1.886	2.920	4.303	6.965	9.925
3	0.765	1.638	2.353	3.182	4.541	5.841
4	0.741	1.533	2.132	2.776	3.747	4.604
5	0.727	1.476	2.015	2.571	3.365	4.032
6	0.718	1.440	1.943	2.447	3.143	3.707
7	0.711	1.415	1.895	2.365	2.998	3.499
8	0.706	1.397	1.860	2.306	2.896	3.355
9	0.703	1.383	1.833	2.262	2.821	3.250
10	0.700	1.372	1.812	2.228	2.764	3.169
11	0.697	1.363	1.796	2.201	2.718	3.106
12	0.695	1.356	1.782	2.179	2.681	3.055

13	0.694	1.350	1.771	2.160	2.650	3.012
14	0.692	1.345	1.761	2.145	2.624	2.977
15	0.691	1.341	1.753	2.131	2.602	2.947
16	0.690	1.337	1.746	2.120	2.583	2.921
17	0.689	1.333	1.740	2.110	2.567	2.898
18	0.688	1.330	1.734	2.101	2.552	2.878
19	0.688	1.328	1.729	2.093	2.539	2.861
20	0.687	1.325	1.725	2.086	2.528	2.845
21	0.686	1.323	1.721	2.080	2.518	2.831
22	0.686	1.321	1.717	2.074	2.508	2.819
23	0.685	1.319	1.714	2.069	2.500	2.807
24	0.685	1.318	1.711	2.064	2.492	2.797
25	0.684	1.316	1.708	2.060	2.485	2.787
26	0.684	1.315	1.706	2.056	2.479	2.779
27	0.684	1.314	1.703	2.052	2.473	2.771
28	0.683	1.313	1.701	2.048	2.467	2.763
29	0.683	1.311	1.699	2.045	2.462	2.756
30	0.683	1.310	1.697	2.042	2.457	2.750
40	0.681	1.303	1.684	2.021	2.423	2.704
60	0.679	1.296	1.671	2.000	2.390	2.660
120	0.677	1.289	1.658	1.980	2.358	2.617
°	0.674	1.282	1.645	1.960	2.326	2.576

Source: Stat Trek (2007).

APPENDIX 5

Critical Values of the
Chi Square Distribution

df	Level of Significance		
	.05	.025	.01
1	3.84	5.02	6.64
2	5.99	7.38	9.21
3	7.81	9.35	11.34
4	9.49	11.14	13.28
5	11.07	12.83	15.09
6	12.59	14.45	16.81
7	14.07	16.01	18.48
8	15.51	17.53	20.09
9	16.92	19.02	21.67
10	18.31	20.48	23.21
11	19.68	21.92	24.72
12	21.03	23.34	26.22
13	22.36	24.74	27.69
14	23.68	26.11	29.14

15	25.00	27.49	30.58
16	26.30	28.85	32.00
17	27.59	30.19	33.41
18	28.87	31.53	34.80
19	30.14	32.85	36.19
20	31.41	34.17	37.57
21	32.67	35.48	38.93
22	33.92	36.78	40.29
23	35.17	38.08	41.64
24	36.42	39.36	42.98
25	37.65	40.65	44.31
26	38.88	41.92	45.64
27	40.11	43.19	46.96
28	41.34	44.46	48.28
29	42.56	45.72	49.59
30	43.77	46.98	50.89
40	55.76	59.34	63.69
50	67.50	71.42	76.15
60	79.08	83.29	88.38
70	90.53	95.02	100.42
80	101.88	106.63	100.43
90	113.15	118.14	124.12
100	124.34	129.56	135.81

Source: Stat Trek (2007).

APPENDIX 6

Thesis Cover Template

THE IMPACT OF THE FINANCIAL
SECTOR REFORM ON THE PERFORMANCE
OF BANKING INSTITUTIONS IN KENYA

by

JOHN NJUGUNA

This paper was submitted in partial fulfilment of the requirements for the degree of Master's in Business Administration (MBA)

Awarded by

ESAMI
Eastern & Southern Africa
P. O. BOX 3030
Arusha, TANZANIA

November 2008

Sample Thesis Declaration Statement

DECLARATION

I, Mary Mwansambo, declare that I am the sole author of this dissertation, that during the period of registered study I have not been registered for other academic award or qualification, nor has any of the material been submitted wholly or partly for any other award. This dissertation is a result of my own research work, and where other people's research was used, they have been dully acknowledged.

Date _____ Signature _____

(CANDIDATE)

Sample MBA Thesis—
The Field Experiment Design
(Quantitative Approach)

Note: Names marked * are fictitious names in the sample thesis.

DOES MICROCREDIT REALLY HELP IN POVERTY ALLEVIATION? A STUDY OF THE IMPACT OF MARDEF LOANS ON POVERTY STATUS OF ITS BENEFICIARIES IN BLANTYRE DISTRICT OF MALAWI

BY

John Phiri*

This paper was submitted in partial fulfilment of the requirements for the award of ESAMI Degree Master's in Business Administration (MBA)

Awarded by

ESAMI
Eastern and Southern Africa
Management Institute
P O Box 3030
Arusha
TANZANIA

November, 2008

DECLARATION

I, John Phiri*, declare that I am the sole author of this dissertation, that during the period of registered study I have not been registered for other academic award or qualification, nor has any of the material been submitted wholly or partly for any other award. This dissertation is a result of my own research work, and where other people's research was used, they have been dully acknowledged.

Date:_____ Signature: _____

(CANDIDATE)

Date: _____ Name: _____

Signature: _____

(SUPERVISOR)

CONTENTS

LIST OF ABBREVIATIONS AND ACRONYMS

ACRONYM	FULL MEANING
MARDEF	Malawi Rural Development Fund
ESAMI	Eastern and Southern Africa Management Institute
MCA	Malawi College of Accountancy
UNDP	United Nations Development Programme
GOM	Government of Malawi
PAP	Poverty Alleviation Programme
WB	World Bank
UNICEF	United Nations International Children Educational Fund
DFID	Development Fund for International Development
GANYU	Piece work for wages

LIST OF FIGURES AND TABLES

ACKNOWLEDGEMENTS

This independent research paper benefited so much from the inputs of many people. To begin with, I would like to thank the principal and management of the Malawi College of Accountancy (MCA) for providing me with the scholarship for the MBA program without which my full intellectual capability would not have been realized. Fellow employees also deserve thanks for willingly assisting me in many ways of my requests for materials and information throughout my MBA studies.

Special thanks are also due to the professors from ESAMI, especially Professor John Martin* who provided valuable guidance in the supervision of this independent research project. I must state that I benefited immensely from the teaching of these world-class lecturers. I also enjoyed sharing work experiences with fellow MBA class members for intake 15 in Malawi under the guidance of the professors.

This work also benefited from the input of individuals from Blantyre district rural who are both MARDEF microcredit beneficiaries and non-beneficiaries. To them I am very grateful for bearing the trauma of narrating their visibly pathetic livelihoods. I sincerely hope that the results of this study can be used by MARDEF, the government of Malawi, and other microcredit institutions in Malawi to help the poor households improve their livelihoods.

I am particularly indebted to the MARDEF Blantyre District project officer who escorted me to various corners of the district during the field data collection stage of this work. Whilst in the field, the project officer linked me so well with MARDEF loan beneficiaries and qualifying non-MARDEF loan beneficiaries for me to successfully conduct the interviews. To the project officer I say thanks for a good job.

Finally, I thank my wife Jane* and daughter Caroline* for their understanding, patience, and encouragement throughout the more than two and half years in which the husband and father was trying to improve his educational qualifications in order to set a pace for the rest of the family members to achieve in life.

ABSTRACT

Poverty remains rampant in Malawi. About 50 per cent of smallholder households are food insecure, and 60 per cent of the rural and 65 per cent of the urban population earn incomes below the poverty line of US $40 per year (Government of Malawi, 2007).

In common with many other developing countries, the Malawi government has over the past few years allocated vast resources towards funding microcredit programs aimed at reducing poverty of the participating households. One such prominent microcredit program is the "5 billion Malawi Kwacha" Malawi Rural Development Fund (MARDEF) which was established in 2004 and operates nationwide. MARDEF was used as a case study in this research.

In spite of the vast microcredit support given to poor households, poverty appears to persist among the receiving households in Malawi. As a result, questions are now arising about the effectiveness of microcredit as a policy intervention to reduce poverty. Does microcredit really help in poverty alleviation among receiving households in the Malawi context? This study was therefore conducted to contribute towards a better understanding of the impact of microcredit programs on poverty alleviation of participating households in Malawi.

The study involved investigating the differences in wealth/poverty levels of a random sample of 84 poor households drawn from six constituencies of Blantyre district rural where MARDEF is operating. Half (42) of the surveyed households (treatment group) were supported with microcredit by MARDEF at its outset in 2004. The other half (42) of the households (control group) had never received loans from MARDEF or any other microcredit institution during the period before the survey. These control households were identified from the "loans waiting list" prepared by MARDEF. It was a fortunate development (from a research point of view) that after disbursing the first loans and pre-identifying the next beneficiaries, the MARDEF program was suspended due to politics and shortage of funds. This made the economic progress of treatment group comparable with those in control group over a four-year period.

Data for comparing wealth level was collected on variables such as: accumulation levels of fixed assets, income levels, production levels, liability levels, education expenses, health service expenses, and food security levels. A questionnaire was designed and administered to the targeted households in the treatment group and control group using face-to-face interviews to collect the data. The analysis of the collected data was done using the Statistical Package for Social scientists (SPSS) to produce inferential statistics such as mean scores and analysis of variance to assist in making decisions about the differences in poverty status between the two studied groups.

Contrary to expectations and the Null hypothesis, the results of the study showed that access to microcredit had no impact on all the variables used to measure poverty levels of the interviewed receiving households in the treatment group. Furthermore, results of statistical tests (t-tests) conducted to compare economic and social welfare progress between the treatment group and control group revealed no statistically significant difference on: accumulation levels of fixed assets, income levels, production levels, labour force employment levels, savings and investment levels, and expenditure levels on education and health services. These results are justifiable because all the respondents in the treatment group explained that the maximum loans, pegged at K10,000.00 or US $70.00 per person, which they received from MARDEF were too little for them to start and run viable businesses that could cope with economic shocks such as high transport costs and inflation, and at the same time generate enough income to improve their wealth status.

In view of the above findings, the study concluded that access to microcredit alone is making a limited impact on reducing the poverty levels of receiving households in the context of Malawi. This conclusion contradicts the current thinking of the Malawi government and the findings of similar studies done in other countries, which have shown that access to microcredit has a positive impact on many variables used to measure economic and social welfare status of poor households.

To improve the effectiveness of microcredit on poverty alleviation of receiving households, it is recommended that MARDEF should increase the amounts of credit disbursed to each household. With the current low credit amounts but high business operational costs, the poor households are failing to run successful businesses while continuing to make payments on the loans.

It is also recommended that MARDEF should change its strategy of disbursing loans. It should identify priority poverty groups (e.g., poultry farmers and vegetable growers) and focus its limited resources on improving the businesses and economic status of these targeted groups instead of overstretching to distribute loan to all constituencies in Malawi at the same time.

Furthermore, it is recommended that the government of Malawi should also encourage cross-sectional collaboration of microcredit institutions operating in rural Malawi in order to increase their impact of disbursing microcredit to reducing poverty receiving households.

Another recommendation is that the Malawi government should intensify civil education aimed at promoting public awareness of the objectives of microcredit programs, particularly the MARDEF loan scheme which has generated misconceptions among poor households. The mind-set of the majority of households, who think MARDEF loans are political campaign money which can be used unproductively, should be changed.

Lastly, it is recommended that the government of Malawi should supplement access to microcredit with inputs for work (*ganyu*) programs to assist poor households to access fertilizers and other inputs which are vital for improving production levels.

CHAPTER 1

RESEARCH BACKGROUND

1.1   INTRODUCTION

This research study is an extension, with some modifications, of the earlier studies on the impact of microcredit on poverty alleviation conducted by Coleman (1999), Khandkar (2003), World Bank (1990), and others in various parts of the world. Results of those studies indicate that microcredit programs have a positive impact on reducing the poverty of the beneficiaries. As a result of the findings, the popular press has waved the banner of microcredit as the most important tool to reduce poverty, (*The Economist*, 1993; *New York Times*, 1997). The 1997 microcredit summit called for the mobilization of US $20 billion over a 10-year period to support microfinance (Microcredit Summit Report, 1997). The United Nations proclaimed 2005 as the "year of microcredit". In Malawi, the government set up in 2005 the largest ever microcredit scheme for the poor worth 5 billion Malawi kwacha, which is known as the Malawi Rural Development Fund (MARDEF).

Much as there has been a lot of faith in microcredit programs, in the case of Malawi, there has been little sound empirical research that has tested the hypothesis that microcredit positively reduces the poverty of its beneficiaries to justify the significant investments government is making in microcredit programs (Government of Malawi, 1995). In fact, prominent dissenters to the belief in microcredit have written that most Malawians are too poor to be able to benefit from any kind of access to credit and that even if they had access to adequate credit and inputs, their land constraints are so severe that any increase in productivity will still fall short of guaranteeing poverty reduction (Diagne and Zeller, 2001). Consequently, the objective of this research is to gain better understanding on the relationship between microcredit programs and

189

poverty alleviation in the case of Malawi using the 5 billion kwacha MARDEF microcredit program as the case study.

1.2   BACKGROUND OF THE MALAWI RURAL DEVELOPMENT FUND (MARDEF)

As mentioned in the introduction, the microcredit scheme which is the focus of this research study is known as the Malawi Rural Development Fund (MARDEF), and it is administered in all the twenty-eight districts of Malawi. The loan scheme, whose target is to lend up to 5 billion Malawi kwacha to the poor, was launched by the president, Dr Bingu wa Mutharika on January 29, 2005. It has been operational for three years.

According to MARDEF (2005), the objective of the 5 billion kwacha loan scheme is "to assist those Malawians who wish to set up small businesses in the country by providing them with financial means of setting up new businesses or expanding old ones." The fund particularly targets women and youth as main beneficiaries, although men also benefit from it. The fund is of a revolving nature and its continuity is therefore dependent on timely repayments of the loans by borrowers (MARDEF, 2005).

MARDEF has its head office in Lilongwe, the capital city of Malawi. Its organizational structure consists of a board of directors, management, and staff. The board is appointed by the Minister of Finance and is responsible for giving policy direction for the management and administration of the fund's affairs. The management and staff deal with the implementation of policies and operational issues of the fund (MARDEF, 2005).

MARDEF uses social collateral in the form of peer groups to ensure loan repayments. In this regard, prospective beneficiaries form groups through a self-selecting process with the aim of carrying out viable businesses that can lead to alleviation of their poverty. Within a group, loans are extended to either an individual member of the group, to subgroups that belong to one enterprise, or to the whole group of members belonging to one enterprise. Where a member fails to repay the loan, the entire group typically is penalized, and each member is barred altogether from taking further loans. This peer pressure is used to encourage borrowers to repay the loans, (MARDEF, 2005).

Preferred business ventures that are considered for funding are those in line with the fund's aim of encouraging productive enterprises for poverty alleviation, such as fish, poultry, and dairy farming, baking of confectionaries, bee-keeping, vegetable growing, fruit juice production, cane furniture, etc. Only projects or businesses that are considered to be financially viable and capable of generating profits are approved (MARDEF, 2005).

Interest on the loans is 15 per cent or the prime commercial bank rate less 5 per cent, whichever is lower, levied on a straight-line basis. For short-term businesses the repayment period is twelve months, inclusive of a grace period of three months.

Medium-term businesses, such as dairy farming, egg production, fish farming, etc., are given longer grace periods, and the repayment is more than twelve months. Instalments for loan repayment are paid monthly. The initial minimum loan amount per individual in a group is K10,000.00, while the maximum is MK100,000.00, and such amounts increase proportionally in group lending (MARDEF, 2005).

1.3   STATEMENT OF THE RESEARCH PROBLEM

In the past few years, microcredit for the poor has received extensive recognition by the Malawi government as the most important tool to reduce poverty (Government of Malawi's Poverty Reduction Strategy paper, 2004). The recent effort by the Malawi government to set up the 5 billion kwacha Malawi Rural Development Fund (MARDEF) on July 29, 2005 is inspired largely by the belief that such microcredit schemes reach the poor and have positive impacts on their poverty alleviation (MARDEF, 2005). As stated in the introduction, much of this faith in microcredit is based on research findings conducted in other parts of the world which reported to have found evidence of individuals who have pulled themselves and their families out of poverty with the benefit of microcredit.

In countries such as Bangladesh, India, Peru, and Ethiopia, studies conducted by the World Bank have shown that microcredit programs on average and in general do have a positive and social economic impact on the poor, although the effects are often small (World Bank, 1990). This finding is supported by Khandkar (2003) who reports that "microcredit matters a lot to the poor in raising per capital consumption, mainly on non-food as well as household non-land assets. This increases the probability that microcredit program participants may be able to lift themselves out of poverty." Khandkar (2003) also finds that microcredit has a village-level "spill-over" effect, reducing extreme poverty even among non-participants.

However, other researchers disagree with the above study findings and report that microcredit is too limited to alleviate poverty in general, especially in societies where many causes other than restricted access to credit have resulted in impoverishment (Karen Mre, 1990).

This observation is supported by Adams and Von Pischke (1992), who have written that "debt is not an effective tool for helping most poor people enhance their economic condition—be they operators of small farms or micro-entrepreneurs or poor women."They argue that access to credit is not a significant problem faced by small agricultural households and that factors such as product prices, land tenure, technology, and risk are the ones limiting small farmer development.

Given the above mixed debate on the role of microcredit in poverty alleviation by previous researchers and to justify the substantial investment which the Malawi Government is making in microcredit to reduce poverty such as the setting up of the 5 billion kwacha microcredit scheme (compared to alternative investments in other poverty alleviation programs), the proposition that microcredit reaches the poor and positively reduces their poverty should be proven and not just assumed. Consequently, this research study is inspired to conduct further research to prove or reject the popular view that microcredit programs have a positive significant impact on poverty alleviation.

1.4   RESEARCH QUESTIONS

1.   What are the economic and social measuring variables which have a bearing on poverty alleviation, according to literature?
2.   Does access to microcredit have any significant positive impact on the economic and social measuring variables of poverty in the case of Malawi?

1.5   RESEARCH OBJECTIVES

From the above research question, the main objectives of the study are:

1.   To identify the main economic and social measuring variables that have a bearing on poverty alleviation.
2.   To evaluate the impact of the MARDEF microcredit program on the various economic and social measures of poverty of its beneficiaries in Blantyre district of Malawi.
3.   After understanding the relationship between microcredit and poverty alleviation, to be able to make policy recommendations on whether the Malawi government should continue relying

on access to microcredit by the poor as an important tool to reduce poverty in the country.

1.6   RESEARCH HYPOTHESES

A hypothesis is some testable belief or opinion. Consequently, hypothesis testing is the process by which the belief is tested by statistical means. The Null hypothesis designated H_o is the one which is tested. If it is found to be true, H_o is accepted, while if H_o is found to be false, it is rejected and an Alternative hypothesis designated H_1 is accepted (Lucey, 1996). In this study the Null hypothesis and Alternative hypotheses are as follows.

The Null hypothesis (H_o) is that there is a significant positive relationship between access to microcredit and poverty reduction of the beneficiaries in the case of Malawi. This assertion is based on the findings of previous studies by Coleman (2006), Khandkar (2003), and World Bank (1990) and others who reported to have found evidence of a positive relationship between microcredit and poverty alleviation.

The Alternative hypothesis (H_1) is that there is no significant positive relationship between access to microcredit and poverty reduction of the beneficiaries in Malawi.

1.7   THEORETICAL FRAMEWORK

A theoretical framework is a collection of interrelated concepts which guides the research study in determining what things to measure and what statistical relationship to look for (Chinyanga, 2007). In this study, the theoretical framework used by Coleman (2006) in evaluating the impact of microcredit in Northern Thailand is adopted and used. Coleman (2006) identified ten important measures of economic and social welfare that can give a positive impact on poverty alleviation. The measures are physical assets levels and amounts, income levels, savings and investment levels, debts, production levels, sales, employment levels, health care expenses, education expenses and food security.

Figure 1 provides a diagram showing the relationship between independent and dependent variables according to Coleman (2006). Basically, the diagram shows that **access to microcredit** (as an independent variable) impacts **poverty alleviation**(the dependent variables) measured by changes in: physical assets levels and amounts, income levels, savings levels, debts, production levels, sales, employment levels, healthcare expenses, education expenses, and food security.

FIGURE 1: RELATIONSHIP BETWEEN ACCESS TO MICROCREDIT AND POVERTY ALLEVIATION.

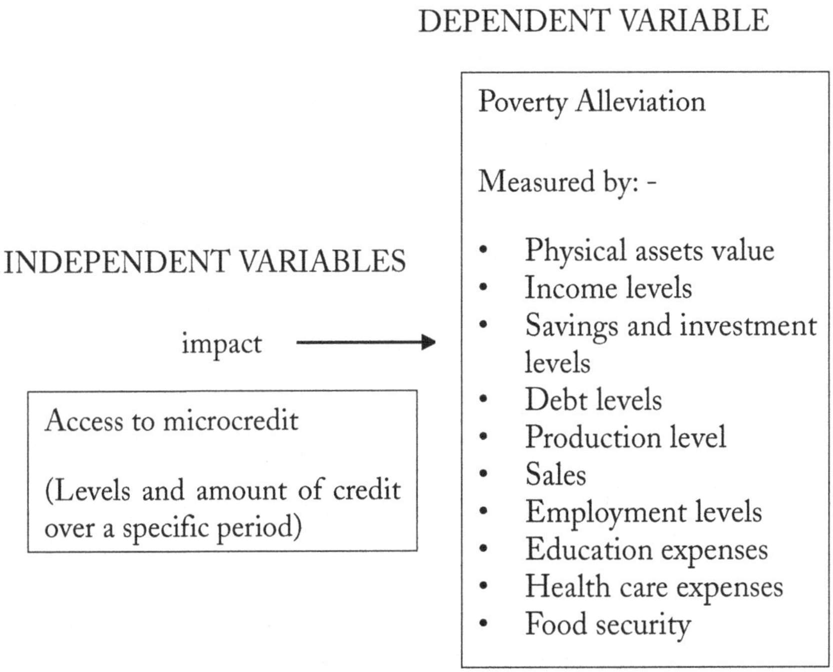

DEPENDENT VARIABLE

INDEPENDENT VARIABLES

impact ⟶

Access to microcredit
(Levels and amount of credit over a specific period)

Poverty Alleviation
Measured by: -
• Physical assets value • Income levels • Savings and investment levels • Debt levels • Production level • Sales • Employment levels • Education expenses • Health care expenses • Food security

CHAPTER 2

LITERATURE REVIEW

2.0 INTRODUCTION

As mentioned in the introduction and problem statement of this research paper, the interest to study the impact of microcredit on poverty alleviation has arisen because of the findings and debate on the link between microcredit and poverty by previous researchers in other parts of the world. Before reviewing the theory behind the linking of microcredit to poverty alleviation and the findings of empirical studies, it is necessary to define the terms "microcredit" and "poverty" to gain a better understanding of their meaning in this study.

Microcredit is defined as credit services appropriate to and accessible by poor and low-income people who are generally denied access to formal financial system credit on sustainable basis following best practices (Malawi Government, 1999). On the other hand, poverty is defined as the lack of basic needs and resources in terms of money, food, shelter, clothes, access to education, health care, and employment, among others (Malawi Government, 2001). It is in the interest of this study to examine how microcredit impacts on poverty alleviation.

2.1 IMPACT OF MICROCREDIT ON ERADICATION OF POVERTY

Theoretically, it is generally agreed among authors and policy makers that poor households in developing countries lack adequate access to credit. This lack of adequate access to credit is in turn believed to have significant negative consequence for various aggregate and household-level outcomes, including asset ownership, income levels, technology adoption, productivity, food security, education, health, and overall household welfare (Zeller et al., 1997).

A number of previous researchers have found that access to microcredit has a positive impact on various measures of poverty as follows:

a) Impact on Asset Ownership

Dunn (2001), studying the impact of microcredit in Peru, observed that microcredit programs have a positive impact on the accumulation of assets by the beneficiary group. The study results show that the microcredit beneficiaries group accumulated US $500 more in assets than did enterprises in the control group (non-beneficiaries).

Khandkar (2003:4) agrees with Dunn (2001) that microcredit programmes help the poor to build up assets. He found that in Bangladesh poor women who had access to microcredit were able to acquire assets of their own, and therefore he reported that "microcredit matters a lot to the poor in raising per capita consumption, mainly on non-food as well as non-land assets." This increases the probability that microcredit program participants may be able to lift themselves out of poverty.

Hulme (1990) subscribes to Dunn's and Khandkar's arguments and further writes that assets have at least three main roles in eradication of poverty as follows:

(i)   They can generate an income and benefit flow to meet the present needs of the poor.
(ii) They can generate a surplus so that more assets can be accumulated.
(iii) They can be used as a buffer to reduce vulnerability and cope with shocks and stresses.

b) Impact on Income Levels

Another way in which microcredit programs can contribute to the eradication of poverty is by increasing income levels of the poor, (United Nations, 2005). The study conducted by the United Nations (2005) in Latin America, Asia, and Kenya revealed that microcredit programs have positive impacts on poor households' income. For example, in Latin America, it was found that given some 1997 income levels, the treatment (beneficiary) group households were estimated to have US $1,200 more in 1999 annual income and US $266 more in per capita income (both in real terms) than comparable control group households (non-beneficiaries). Put in context, a US $266 increase in per capita income represents more than 20 per cent of the average per capita income of the sample. These impacts on income are attributed to growth in enterprise revenue, which would indicate that microcredit-driven changes in enterprises result in improvements in poor household welfare (United Nations, 2005).

c) Impact on Production

Hulme (1990) found that microcredit programs provide additional capital to poor households. This additional capital can be used to enhance the level of the household's productive human and physical capital (that is, learn skills, hire workers, rent land, purchase tools and inputs, etc.)

Zeller et al (1997) agrees with Hulme (1990) and writes that access to microcredit reduces the poverty of beneficiaries through alleviation of capital constraints on business and agricultural production. For example, in agricultural production, expenditures on inputs and on food and essential non-food items are incurred during the planting and vegetable growth period of crops, whereas returns are received only after the crops are harvested several months later. Most farming households show a negative cash flow during the planting season. Therefore, to finance the purchase of essential consumption and production inputs, household must either dig into its savings or obtain credit. Access to microcredit therefore significantly increases the ability of poor households with little or no savings to acquire agriculture inputs and increase production (Zeller et al 1997).

d) Impact on Savings and Investments

Eswaran and Kotwal (1990) argue that microcredit programs play a positive role in increasing a household's ability to save and invest in different types of profitable business ventures. The mere access to microcredit may induce a poor household to adopt new, riskier technologies and investments which may yield income and social welfare.

A study conducted by the International Fund for Agriculture Development (IFAD) in 2000 in Northern Ghana, Nigeria and other African countries confirmed the positive role of microcredit programs in increasing savings and investment of poor people. The IFAD study found that in many developing countries, capital markets are still at rudimentary stage, and commercial banks are reluctant to lend to the poor, largely because of the lack of collateral and high transaction costs. Therefore, the availability of small loans allows the poor people to introduce small enterprises which generates higher and more stable incomes, savings and further investments (IFAD, 2000).

e) Impact on Employment

Dunn (2001) found that microcredit programs have a positive impact on employment of the poor household beneficiaries. In her study on the impact of microcredit programs in Peru, Dunn (2001) observed that households receiving microcredit provided about nine more days of total employment per month and 3.25 more days of paid employment per month for non-household members than households not receiving microcredit.

Hulme (1990) agrees with Dunn (2001) that microcredit programs have a positive impact on employment of poor people. Hulme observed that by providing opportunities for self-employment, microcredit programs have significantly increased poor women's security, self-confidence, and status within their households.

f) Impact on Social Welfare (Empowerment, Education Attainment, and Health Care)

Zeller et al (1997) found that access to microcredit impacts positively on various measures of welfare. He observed that access to microcredit enabled poor people to increase their medical and school expenses for children and other household members. With improved access to education and health care, illiteracy and disease will reduce significantly, and therefore poverty will be reduced (Zeller et al, 1997).

Khandkar (2003) agrees with Zeller et al (1997) and argues that microcredit programs promote investments in human capital, such as schooling, and increase awareness of reproductive health, such as use of contraceptives among poor families.

Coleman (2006), studying the impact of microcredit on poverty alleviation in northeast Thailand, also agrees with Zeller et al (1997) and Khandkar (2003) that microcredit programs have a positive impact on social welfare. As such, Coleman (2006) argues that although the initial objectives of microcredit was not primarily, in the "social" realm, evidence has been found of positive impact on women's empowerment, children school attendance, awareness and demand for health services, etc.

Arguably, due to the above evidence, which shows that microcredit does have a positive impact on poverty alleviation, it is difficult to find a poverty reduction strategy that does include microcredit as a main element of national strategy for poverty alleviation, (Hulme, 1990).

2.2 CONTRADICTORY EMPIRICAL EVIDENCE ON IMPACT OF MICROCREDIT ON ERADICATION OF POVERTY

Other researchers disagree with the above findings that microcredit programs have a positive impact on the various economic and social measures of poverty. They argue that microcredit is too limited to alleviate poverty in general, especially in societies where many causes other than restricted access to credit have resulted in impoverishment, (Karen Mre, 1990).

Adams and Von Pischke (1992) agree with Karen Mre (1990) and write that "debt is not an effective tool for helping most poor people enhance their economic condition—be they operators of small farms or micro entrepreneurs or poor women." They argue that access to credit is not a significant problem faced by small agricultural households and that product prices, land tenure, technology, and risk are the factors limiting small farmers' development.

In his study, Gina Neff (1996) also disagrees with the popular findings of other researchers that microcredit has a positive impact on poverty alleviation. He argues that the success of the microcredit model has been judged disproportionately from the lender's perspective (repayment rates, financial viability) and not from that of the borrower. For example, the Grameen Bank's high repayment rate does not reflect the number of women who are repeat borrowers and have become dependent on loans for household expenditure rather than capital investments.

Another study of microcredit programs has found that the need for profitable micro-lending by micro-finance institutions shifts microcredit to those who are less poor and have the capacity to repay loans while failing to lend to the very poorest who appear not to have resources or capacity to repay the loans, (Meade, 2001).

Other studies have also revealed that most poor people require small loans because they avoid the risk of big loan repayments. This habit makes them undertake enterprises which run with small stocks, and hence they make marginal profits. The marginal profit is then shared between household needs and business continuity, and little or no money is left for savings and re-investment, and hence poverty continues (Still 1998; IFAD 2000; Zaman 2001).

2.3.1 IMPACT OF MICROCREDIT ON POVERTY ALLEVIATION: THE CASE STUDY OF MALAWI

In the case of Malawi, previous research studies specifically on the impact of microcredit on poverty alleviation are rare. However, there has been one notable major effort by Alion Diagne and Manfred Zeller (2001), who researched on a related but different topic, namely "Access to credit and its impact on net crop income as a measure of welfare in Malawi" published in Research Report 116 by International Food Policy Research Institute, Washington DC in 2001. The main finding of the study is that there is a negative (albeit insignificant) relationship between borrowing and net crop income and welfare.

From the above presented theoretical work and mixed findings of empirical studies conducted in other parts of the world and the shortage of literature on the subject in Malawi, it is clear that there is need to conduct further research on the subject to test the hypothesis that microcredit programs, particularly the Malawi Rural Development Fund, are benefiting the poor. The next chapter discusses the methodology to be used in the study.

CHAPTER 3

RESEARCH METHODOLOGY

3.1   RESEARCH APPROACH AND STRATEGY

The standard practice in previous studies on the impact of microcredit on poverty alleviation has been to measure the differences on various economic measures of welfare such as wealth and income and social measures such as educational attainment and health status between the loan beneficiaries and non-beneficiaries (Coleman, 2006; Zeller et al, 1996; World Bank, 1990). The same model will be adopted and used in this study.

Using the above standard practice, this study involved investigating the differences in wealth/poverty levels of a random sample of 84 poor households drawn from six constituencies of Blantyre district rural where MARDEF is operating. Half (42) of the surveyed households (treatment group) were supported with microcredit by MARDEF at its outset in 2004. The other half (42) of the households (control group) had never received loans from MARDEF or any other microcredit institution during the period before the survey. These control households were identified from the "loans waiting list" prepared by MARDEF.

A sample size of 42 households in the treatment group and another 42 households in the control group was considered reasonable and acceptable in this research study, because it was above the recommended number of 30 respondents and therefore represented the majority of the population (Chinyanga, 2007).

It was also a fortunate development (from a research point of view) that after disbursing the first loans and pre-identifying next beneficiaries, the MARDEF program was suspended due to politics and shortage of funds. This made the economic progress of the treatment group comparable with those in the control group over a four-year period.

3.2   COLLECTION OF DATA

As discussed in the Theoretical Framework of this study, data was collected from both MARDEF loan beneficiaries and non-MARDEF loan beneficiaries using the questionnaire presented in Appendix 1. Using this questionnaire, data was mainly collected from poverty reduction measuring variables such as: accumulation of fixed assets, income levels, production levels, savings and investment levels, employment levels, food security levels, and expenditure on educational and health services as shown in Table 1.

3.3   USE OF CHECKLIST FOR VERIFYING ACCURANCY OF INFORMATION PROVIDED BY RESPONDENTS.

Before conducting the face-to-face interviews with respondents, the researcher visited three markets in the targeted study areas and collected data on market prices of common assets owned by households (see Appendix 1). The purpose of collecting the data on market prices was to use it in cross-checking the accuracy of information on market prices/values of assets provided by interviewed households.

Table 1: Research Variables to Measure the Impact
of MARDEF Loans on Poverty Alleviation

POVERTY ALLEVIATION MEASURING VARIABLE	TREATMENT GROUP (BENEFICIARIES OF MARDEF LOANS)	CONTROL GROUP NON BENEFICIARIES OF MARDEF LOANS
ACCUMULATION OF FIXED ASSETS		
TYPE OF ASSET OWNED (Value in Malawi Kwacha)		
• All assets	K	K
• Land	K	K
• Productive assets (buildings, equipment)	K	K
• Non production assets (furniture, utensils)	K	K
• Livestock (cattle, goats, chicken)	K	K
• Other assets	K	K
INCOME LEVELS PER ANNUM SOURCE OF INCOME		
• Crop sales	K	K
• Livestock sales	K	K
• Self-employment	K	K
• Wage employment	K	K

• Business Sales	K	K
• Credit	K	K
• Other sources	K	K
SAVINGS AND INVESTMENTS PER ANNUM		
• Cash savings	K	K
• Assets investments/ bought	K	K
LIABILITIES/DEBT STATUS TYPE OF DEBT		
• Household internal borrowing	K	K
• MARDEF debt	K	K
• Debt from banks/ microcredit institutions	K	K
• Debt from other lenders	K	K
PRODUCTION LEVELS PER ANNUM (Measured in Malawi kwacha)		
• Crop production for sales	K	K
• Crop production for consumption	K	K

• Animal production for sales	K	K
• Animal production for consumption	K	K
• Business production	K	K
EXPENSES (in Malawi kwacha)		
• Household expenses	K	K
• Crop production for consumption	K	K
• Animal production for consumption	K	K
• Business production	K	K
ACCESS TO EDUCATION		
• School expenses for children in households	K	K
• Training expenses for self and spouse	K	K
• School expense for relatives	K	K
ACCESS TO HEALTH CARE		
• Medical expenses for self	K	K

• Medical expenses made for children	K	K
• Medical expenses made for other household members	K	K
FOOD SECURITY • Meals per day (average)	K	K
EMPLOYMENT LEVELS • Household labourers, including owner	K	K
• Other external labourers	K	K

The above primary data was collected during the face-to-face interviews between the researcher and the MARDEF loan beneficiaries and non-beneficiaries. As already stated above, the main tool for data collection was a researcher-administered structured questionnaire presented in Appendix 1. In the questionnaire, the questions are a mixture of open-ended and closed questions. Both qualitative and quantitative data was collected.

The face-to-face research technique was chosen among other methods, such as mail surveys and telephone surveys, because the majority of MARDEF loan beneficiaries have too low an education to read, understand, and complete self-administered questionnaires. In addition, a telephone survey would not have worked properly because most of the respondents have no access to telephones. On the other hand, the mail-survey technique was not selected because it yields low response, (Chinyanga, 2007). In addition, the postal services in Malawi are known for their inefficiencies, and this could have delayed the research process.

Secondary sources were also used in this research. This is so because secondary sources were equally important in increasing the researcher's knowledge on the subject of microcredit and poverty and in identifying the methods and approaches used by other researchers in similar studies and also in identifying gaps in the knowledge (Chinyanga, 2007). In this regard, the secondary data sources used in this study included books, magazines, research papers and electronic journals sourced from the internet.

3.4   AREAS OF STUDY

Blantyre district was selected for this study. This is so because this district was close to the researcher's working place in the city of Blantyre, and the researcher found it easy and cheaper to travel to the identified study areas. MARDEF loans are distributed to all parliamentary constituencies in Malawi, including the following areas that were covered by the survey in Blantyre district rural:

BLANTYRE: Blantyre North constituency, Blantyre North East constituency Blantyre, Rural East constituency, Blantyre South West constituency, Blantyre City Central constituency and Blantyre Malabada constituency.

3.5   PILOT STUDY

Before the questionnaire was administered, a pilot study was conducted. A small pilot sample of 10% of the treatment group (MARDEF loan beneficiaries) and also 10% of the control group (non-beneficiaries) was interviewed. The purpose of this pilot study was to check if the questions in the questionnaire were simple, clear, useful, and necessary to meet the objectives of the study. Ambiguities, inconsistencies, and deficiencies in the design of questions and content of the questionnaire that were identified were corrected accordingly before the questionnaire was administered to the respondents in the main survey.

3.6   DATA COLLECTION PERIOD

Primary data was collected from June 22, 2008 and July 16, 2008. The advantage of collecting data during this period was that it was after the rainy season in the southern region of Malawi, and it was easy for the researcher to reach all the targeted study areas in Blantyre district.

3.7   DATA ANALYSIS

Using the Statistical Package for Social Scientists software, quantitative data collected from the questionnaires was analysed, mainly through descriptive and inferential statistics. The descriptive statistics, such as the mean, were used to assist the researcher in describing and comparing variables numerically. Inferential statistics such as Analysis of Variance (ANOVA) and t-test were also used to make judgments of significant levels of the findings at $p<.05$ about a population on the basis of a sample used in the study.

3.8   RESEARCH ETHICS

Throughout the research, confidentiality and privacy of the respondents was strictly observed. Respondents were allowed to voluntarily participate in the study. The researcher did not use any force to get information from MARDEF loan beneficiaries and non-beneficiaries. An introduction letter from ESAMI regarding the study was be made available to all respondents. In addition, the researcher explained the purpose of the study to all the respondents before commencing the face-to-face interviews.

3.9   LIMITATIONS OF THE RESEARCH METHODOLOGY

The study methodology used had the following limitations:

1. The study covered only one district in the Southern region of Malawi out of twenty-eight districts of the country benefiting from 5 billion kwacha MARDEF loan scheme. The results might not be a true representation of the information on the ground in other districts.

2. MARDEF District Credit Officers had the knowledge of the areas where interviews were conducted. This was so because visits were pre-arranged to enable respondents gather at destined locations for convenience. Officer's knowledge of the planned visits might have compromised answers to questions provided by respondents.

3. Lack of accurate accounting records by respondents made it difficult for the researcher to collect accurate data. The researcher had to rely on oral and recall information provided by respondents. In many cases it was difficult to verify business transactions in terms accumulation levels of fixed assets, income levels, production levels, business sales, profits, savings, liabilities and expenditure levels on education and social services.

CHAPTER 4

MAIN FINDINGS AND DISCUSSIONS

4.1   INTRODUCTION

This chapter presents the findings of the survey on the impact of microcredit on various poverty measuring variables. Impact results are presented below under the headings of accumulation of fixed assets, income levels, production levels, savings and investment levels, and food security levels, education and health expenses.

4.2   IMPACT OF MARDEF LOANS ON ACCUMULATION OF FIXED ASSETS BY HOUSEHOLDS IN THE TREATMENT GROUP

As stated in the Research Methodology section, the impact of MARDEF loans on poverty alleviation was assessed by comparing levels of accumulation of fixed assets such as land, productive and non-productive assets, and livestock between the treatment group and the control group. The decision rule was: If it was found that the treatment group had accumulated more fixed assets than the control group during the studied period, January 2004 to July 2008, then this was reliable evidence that access to microcredit contributed to the accumulation of fixed assets by the receiving households.

4.2.1   Results of Comparison of Landholdings between Treatment Group and Control Group

Table 2 presents the results of comparison of landholdings between the treatment group and control group.

Table 2: Comparison of Landholdings between Treatment Group and Control Group

Parcel of Land	Treatment Group		Control Group	
Hectors	% of households	Estimated Value (MK)	% of households	Estimated Value (MK)
<0.5	45	996,682	47	1,018,349
0.5 < 1.0	24	760,008	21	665,007
1.0 < 1.5	17	680,000	18	720,000
1.5 < 2.0	14	676,662	14	676,662
> 2.0	0	0	0	0
Totals	100	3,113,352	100	3,080,018

Source: Research Findings

An analysis of Table 2 reveals that the treatment group had accumulated slightly more land in value by MK3,3334.00. However, this difference was too small to be relied on for meaningful conclusions. Furthermore, Table 2 shows that over 65% of the households in both groups were holding less than 1.0 hectares of land, which is an indication that there were no reliable differences in poverty status between the treatment group and the control group. These findings necessitated further investigations to determine if there was a statistically significant difference in landholdings values and poverty status between the treatment group and the control group. In this regard, a t-Test would indicate if there was significant difference in landholdings values between the two studied groups.

T-Test for Market Value of Land Owned Between Treatment Group and Control Group using SPSS

Levene's Test for Equality of Variances was conducted to investigate if the difference in market value of landholdings between the treatment group and the control group was statistically significant. The Null hypothesis and Alternate hypothesis were:

H_0 = There was no significant difference.
H_1 ≠ There was significant difference.

The decision rule was: If p-value was less than or equal to Alpha (0.05), then reject H_o. The results of the t-test are presented in Appendix 2, Table 3.

Table 3 shows that $t(0.05, 82) = 0.333, p = 0.740$. Since p-value (0.740) is greater than 0.05, then we fail to reject the Null hypothesis (H_0) in line with the decision rule. Therefore we conclude that there was no significant difference in market value of land owned between households in the treatment group and control group.

Furthermore, the mean market value of land for households in the treatment group ($M = 25754.17$, SD = 12910.94) was small and not significantly different from that of households in the control group ($M = 24801.79$, SD = 13303.79). Any minor differences could be attributed to random chance (not statistically significant).

In view of the above results, it is concluded that an equal variances t-test has failed to reveal a statistically reliable difference between landholding values of the treatment group and the control group. Therefore, no evidence has been found to substantiate the fact that microcredit has an impact on acquisition and ownership of more land by receiving households.

Table 3: Results of T-Test for Market Value of Land Owned.

Group Statistics

	Treatment and Control Group	N	Mean	Std. Deviation	Std. Error Mean
Market value of land owned	treatment group	42	25754.17	12910.938	1992.201
	control group	42	24801.79	13303.789	2052.819

Independent Samples Test

		Levene's Test for Equality of Variances		t-test for Equality of Means					95% Confidence Interval of the Difference	
		F	Sig.	T	Df	P-value (Sig. 2-tailed)	Mean Difference	Std. Error Difference	Lower	Upper
Market value of land owned	Equal variances assumed	.003	.960	.333	82	.740	952.38	2860.582	-4738.229	6642.991
	Equal variances not assumed			.333	81.926	.740	952.38	2860.582	-4738.305	6643.067

Source: Data Analysis Output

4.3.2 Results of Comparison of Holdings of Productive and Non-Productive Assets between Treatment Group and Control Group

The results of the survey presented in Table 4 indicate a marginal difference in quantities and value of productive and non-productive assets owned by the treatment group and the control group. Total value of productive and non-productive assets for the treatment group was estimated at a slightly higher value of MK168,008.00 compared to MK153,396.00 for the control group, resulting in a small difference of MK14,612.00 only. Therefore, it was clear from Table 4 that there was no significant differences between the treatment group and the control group in accumulation of productive and non-productive assets.

Table 4: Comparison of Accumulation of Other Productive and Non-Productive Assets between the Treatment Group and the Control Group.

Type of Asset	Treatment Group			Control Group		
	No. of Households	No. of Assets	Estimated Value (MK)	No. of Households	No. of Assets	Estimated Value(MK)
Productive Assets						
Bicycle	22	22	95,326	20	20	86,660
Hoes	38	3	36,562	34	3	23,766
Pangas	20	1	3,000	23	1	3,450
Business Building	2	2	1,132	4	4	2,264
Subtotal	82		126,020	81		116,140
Non-Productive Assets						
Dwelling House	6	6	3,600	8	8	4,800
Furniture	36	1	35,388	32		31,456
Utensils	42		3,000	38		3,000
Subtotal	84		41,988	78		39,256
Grand Total			168,008			153,396

Source: Research Findings.

To investigate if the difference in market value of productive assets and non-productive assets owned by the treatment group and control group was statistically significant, Levene's Test for Equality of Variances was conducted. The Null hypothesis and Alternate hypothesis were:

H_0 = There was no significant difference.
H_1 ≠ There was significant difference.

The decision rule was: If p-value was less than or equal to Alpha (0.05), then reject H_0. The results of the t-test are presented in Appendix 2, Table 5.

Table 5 shows that t (0.05, 82) = 0.490, p = 0.625. Since p-value (0.625) is greater than 0.05, then we fail to reject the Null hypothesis (H_0) in line with the decision rule. Therefore we conclude that there was no significant difference in market value of productive and non-productive assets owned between households in the treatment group and control group.

Furthermore, the mean market value of productive and non-productive assets for households in the treatment group (M = 3732, SD = 1140) was small and therefore not significantly different from that of households in the control group (M = 3845 SD = 977). Any minor differences could be attributed to random chance (not statistically significant).

In view of the above results, it is concluded that an equal variances t-test has failed to reveal a statistically reliable difference between market values of productive and non-productive assets accumulated by the treatment group and the control group. Therefore, no evidence has been found to substantiate the theory that microcredit has an impact on accumulation and ownership of productive and non-productive assets by receiving households

Table 5: Results of T-Test for Market Value of Productive Assets and Non-Productive Assets

Group Statistics

	Treatment and Control Group	N	Mean	Std. Deviation	Std. Error Mean
Market value of nonproductive assets	treatment group	42	3731.50	1140.243	175.943
	control group	42	3845.10	977.357	150.809

Independent Samples Test

		Levene's Test for Equality of Variances		t-test for Equality of Means						
		F	Sig.	T	Df	P-value (Sig. 2-tailed)	Mean Difference	Std. Error Difference	95% Confidence Interval of the Difference	
									Lower	Upper
Market value of nonproductive assets	Equal variances assumed	.998	.321	-.490	82	.625	-113.60	231.732	-574.583	347.393
	Equal variances not assumed			-.490	80.126	.625	-113.60	231.732	-574.745	347.554

Source: Data Analysis Output

4.3.3 Results of Comparison of Livestock Ownership Levels between the Treatment Group and the Control Group

An analysis of Table 6 shows no significant differences in the number of livestock held by interviewed households in the treatment group and the control group. For instance, it is noted that over half of households interviewed in both the treatment group (57.14%) and the control group (54.76%) did not own livestock (although most had owned some in the past).

Table 6: Total Number of Livestock Owned
at the Time of the Study

Type of Livestock	Treatment Group			Control Group		
	No. of Households	No. of Livestock	Estimated Value (MK)	No. of Households	No. of Livestock	Estimated Value (MK)
Chicken	14	30	21,000	15	35	24,500
Goats	12	18	54,000	14	19	57,000
Pigs	5	10	11,330	7	13	14,729
Cattle	1	2	200,000	1	1	100,000
Ducks	0	0	0	4	6	3,000
Pigeons	5	21	5,586	7	30	7,980
No livestock Owned	24	0	0	23	0	0
Grand Total			291,916			207,209

Source: Research Findings

To investigate if the difference in the market value of livestock owned by the treatment group and the control group was statistically significant, Levene's Test for Equality of Variances was conducted. The Null hypothesis and Alternate hypothesis were:

H_0 = There was no significant difference
H_1 ≠ There was significant difference

The decision rule was: If the p-value was less than or equal to Alpha (0.05), then reject H_o. The results of the t-test are presented in Appendix 2, Table 7.

Table 7 shows that $t(0.05, 82) = 0.323, p = 0.748$. Since p-value (0.748) is greater than 0.05, then we fail to reject the Null hypothesis (H_0) in line with the decision rule. Therefore, we conclude that there was no significant difference in market value of livestock owned between households in the treatment group and control group.

Furthermore, the mean market value of livestock for households in the treatment group ($M = 6335.64$, SD $= 5326.582$) was small and therefore not significantly different from that of households in the control group ($M = 6754.67$ SD $= 6508.236$). Any minor differences could be attributed to random chance (not statistically significant).

In view of the above results, it is concluded that an equal variances t-test has failed to reveal a statistically reliable difference between the market values of livestock accumulated by the treatment group and the control group. Therefore, no evidence has been found to substantiate the theory that microcredit has an impact on accumulation and ownership of livestock by receiving households.

Nearly a quarter of households in both the treatment group (33.33%) and the control group (39.43%) owned chickens only (Table 7). Other animals owned by both groups were mainly goats, pigs, and pigeon, with very few households holding cattle. This indicates a dependence on livestock as a buffer against food shortages and a major source of income generation. 80% of households from Treatment Group reported that they were unable to buy additional livestock because of the limited amounts of credit provided by MARDEF, which is only K10,000.00. All the households from the control group indicated that they were unable to hold more livestock due to lack of access to credit from MARDEF and other microcredit institutions.

Table 7: Results of T-Test for Market Value of Livestock

Group Statistics

	Treatment and Control Group	N	Mean	Std. Deviation	Std. Error Mean
Market value of livestock	treatment group	42	6335.64	5326.582	821.909
	control group	42	6754.64	6508.236	1004.243

Independent Samples Test

		Levene's Test for Equality of Variances		t-test for Equality of Means						
		F	Sig.	T	Df	P-value (Sig. 2-tailed)	Mean Difference	Std. Error Difference	95% Confidence Interval of the Difference	
									Lower	Upper
Market value of livestock	Equal variances assumed	1.896	.172	-.323	82	.748	-419.00	1297.705	-3000.549	2162.549
	Equal variances not assumed			-.323	78.915	.748	-419.00	1297.705	-3002.061	2164.061

Source: Data Analysis Output

4.3.4 The Impact of Mardef Loans on Income Levels of Households in the Treatment Group

A close observation of the results of the survey presented in Table 8 below reveals that interviewed households in the treatment group reported higher income levels (MK2,451,100.00 per annum) than those in the control group (MK1,955,000.00 per annum).

Table 8: Comparison of Income Levels per Annum between the Treatment Group and the Control Group

Source	Treatment Group		Control Group	
	% of Household involved	Total Income (MK)	% of Household involved	Total Income (MK)
Ganyu	56	690,000	58	670,000
Beer Brewing	40	460,000	38	468,000
Firewood Sales	38	310,000	37	320,000
Handcraft Sales	36	290,000	35	280,000
Grass Sales	31	170,000	33	110,000
Crop Sales	28	40,000	23	39,000
Livestock Sales	24	35,000	20	38,000
Wage Employment	18	20,800	19	19,400
Petty Trade	16	7,800	11	4,200
Relative Assistance	10	7,500	12	6,400
Credit(MARDEF)	100	420,000	0	0
Total		2,451,100		1,955,000

Source: Research Findings

Levene's Test for Equality of Variances was conducted to investigate if the difference in income levels between the treatment group and control group was statistically significant. The Null hypothesis and Alternate hypothesis were:

H_0 = There was no significant difference.
H_1 ≠ There was significant difference.

The decision rule was: If p-value was less than or equal to Alpha (0.05), then reject H_0. The results of the t-test are presented in Appendix 2, Table 9.

Table 9 shows that $t(0.05, 20) = 0.462, p = 0.649$. Since p-value (0.649) is greater than 0.05, then we fail to reject the Null hypothesis (H_0) in line with the decision rule. Therefore, we conclude that there was no significant difference in income levels between households in the treatment group and control group.

Furthermore, the mean income level for households in the treatment group ($M = 25754.17$, $SD = 12910.94$) was small and therefore not significantly different from that of households in the control group ($M = 24801.79$, $SD = 13303.79$). Any minor differences could be attributed to random chance (not statistically significant).

In view of the above results, it is concluded that an equal variances t-test has failed to reveal a statistically reliable difference between income levels of the treatment group and the control group. Therefore, no evidence has been found to substantiate the fact that microcredit has an impact on income levels by receiving households.

As can also be noted from Table 9, the majority of households in both the treatment group and the control group reported that *ganyu* rather than microcredit was their most important source of income during each year. Income from *ganyu* was commonly between K200 and K300 a day depending on the nature of work. Other important sources of income were firewood and handcraft sales. Firewood was sold at K5 to K10 per bundle in Blantyre City. Handcrafts, mainly composed of palm leaf mats and baskets, were sold at K20 per item, and monthly income was up to K3,000.00. It was worth noting that credit from MARDEF is the smallest source of income for the treatment group, and it appears to make a limited contribution to the income levels of individual households. All households interviewed in the treatment group reported that MARDEF loans are insufficient to finance any meaningful business for income generation.

Table 9: Results of T-Test for Income levels

Group Statistics

	Treatment and Control Group	N	Mean	Std. Deviation	Std. Error Mean
Total income received	treatment group	11	222827.27	230304.755	69439.496
	control group	11	177727.27	227325.129	68541.105

Independent Samples Test

		Levene's Test for Equality of Variances		t-test for Equality of Means						
		F	Sig.	T	Df	P-value (Sig. 2-tailed)	Mean Difference	Std. Error Difference	95% Confidence Interval of the Difference	
									Lower	Upper
Total income received	Equal variances assumed	.012	.915	.462	20	.649	45100.00	97569.087	-158425.549	248625.549
	Equal variances not assumed			.462	19.997	.649	45100.00	97569.087	-158427.762	248627.762

Source: Data Analysis Output

4.3   IMPACT OF MARDEF LOANS ON CROP PRODUCTION LEVELS PER ANNUM OF HOUSEHOLDS IN THE TREATMENT GROUP

A comparison of the crop production levels between the treatment group and the control group is presented in Table 10, showing the percentage of households growing each crop, the quantity achieved in a year, and the estimated market value of quantity production in Malawi kwacha.

Table 10: Percentage of Households Growing Each Crop by Quantity and Market Value (in Malawi Kwacha).

Type of Crop	Treatment Group			Control Group		
	No. of Households	Quantity (kg)	Estimated Value (MK)	No. of Households	Quantity (kg)	Estimated Value (MK)
Maize	100	12,600	630,000	100	10,500	525,000
Vegetables	67	84	4,200	65	82	4,095
Cow Peas	58	730	73,080	59	743	74,340
Sweet Potatoes	67	1,125	112,560	64	1,075	107,520
Beans	47	592	59,220	52	655	65,520
Pumpkins	78	982	49,140	75	945	47,250
Cassava	18	150	15,120	19	159	15,960
Sugar Beans	22	184	18,480	23	193	19,320
Groundnuts	35	294	294,000	33	277	277,200
Sugarcane	25	105	10,500	28	117	11,760
Total		16,846	1,266,300		14,746	1,147,965

Source: Research Findings

A close observation of Table 10 shows that the percentage of households involved, the production levels (quantities achieved), and the estimated values in Malawi Kwacha of crops produced by the treatment group and the control group is not significantly different. In order to confirm that there was no significant difference in market value of crops produced between the treatment group and the control group, a statistical test (t-test) was conducted.

To investigate if the difference in market value of crops produced by the treatment group and control group was statistically significant, Levene's Test for Equality of Variances was conducted. The Null hypothesis and Alternate hypothesis were:

H_0 = There was no significant difference.
H_1 ≠ There was significant difference.

The decision rule was: If p-value was less than or equal to Alpha (0.05), then reject H_0. The results of the t-test are presented in Appendix 2, Table 11.

Table 11 shows that $t(0.05, 18) = 0.146, p = 0.886$. Since p-value (0.886) is greater than 0.05, then we fail to reject the Null hypothesis (H_0) in line with the decision rule. Therefore, we conclude that there was no significant difference in market value of crops produced by households in the treatment group and the control group.

Furthermore, the mean market value of crop production for households in the treatment group (M = 126630.00, SD = 196529.510) was small and therefore not significantly different from that of households in the control group (M = 114796.50 SD = 165017.826). Any minor differences could be attributed to random chance (not statistically significant).

In view of the above results, it is concluded that an equal variances t-test has failed to reveal a statistically reliable difference between market values of crops produced by the treatment group and the control group. Therefore, no evidence has been found to substantiate the theory that microcredit has an impact on crop production levels by receiving households in the case of Blantyre district in Malawi.

Although the majority of the interviewed households in both groups grow five or more crops, the reported production levels of each crop is on a small scale, generating insufficient food and inadequate incomes from the sale of crops.

It is interesting to note that the most commonly reported reasons given for low production of crops by the treatment group was insufficient availability of MARDEF credit funds for the households to buy fertilizers, seeds, planting materials, and adequate land for crop production.

In contrast, the most commonly reported reason given for production of crops by the control group was lack of credit facility to enable households buy fertilizer and planting materials and adequate parcels of land for crop production.

Some few households from both the treatment group and the control group revealed that they had access to inputs such as fertilizer and planting material received through the government targeted input distribution program, but the amounts provided to each household were insufficient for their requirements.

Table 11: Results of T-Test for crop production

Group Statistics

	Treatment and Control Group	N	Mean	Std. Deviation	Std. Error Mean
Total Market value of crops	treatment group	10	126630.00	196529.510	62148.088
	control group	10	114796.50	165017.826	52183.218

Independent Samples Test

		Levene's Test for Equality of Variances		t-test for Equality of Means							
		F	Sig.	T	Df	Sig. (2-tailed)	Mean Difference	Std. Error Difference	95% Confidence Interval of the Difference		
										Lower	Upper
Total Market value of crops	Equal variances assumed	.123	.730	.146	18	.886	11833.50	81150.928		-158658.273	182325.273
	Equal variances not assumed			.146	17.477	.886	11833.50	81150.928		-159024.771	182691.771

Source: Data Analysis Output

4.4 IMPACT OF MARDEF LOANS ON SAVINGS AND INVESTMENTS LEVELS OF HOUSEHOLDS IN THE TREATMENT GROUP.

Microcredit appears to have no impact on the accumulation of savings and investments by the receiving households in the treatment group. During the study, interviewed households in both the treatment group and the control group were asked to reveal how they spend their earnings from various sources of income, including microcredit, and the results are presented in Table 12 below.

Table 12: Use of Cash from Various Sources of Income Earned
by the Treatment Group and the Control Group

Use of Cash/ Income	Treatment Group	Control Group
	%age of Households Involved	%age of Households Involved
Maize Purchase	38	40
Fertilizer	21	18
Soap, Salt, Relish	42	42
Starting a Business	10	6
Clothes	9	8
Loan Repayment	15	N/A
Savings	0	0
Investments	0	0

Source: Research Findings

The data analysis presented in Table 12 shows that there is no significant difference in the use of cash from various income sources between the treatment group and the control group. A closer observation of Table 12 shows that the all the interviewed households in both groups did not save or invest their income during the studied period. However, the majority (90% of households in the treatment group and 95% of households in the control group) are spending a larger proportion of their income to purchase maize for food. Generally, much smaller harvests were reported in the 2007/08 year in all areas covered by the research, with many households reporting no harvest at all. Maximum harvests reported were 8 bags for the treatment group and six bags for the control group.

All the households interviewed in both the treatment group and the control group reported use of their income to buy soap, salt, and relish. A few households in both groups used the cash to buy fertilizer and clothes. Interestingly, only 10% of households from the treatment group reported using their income mainly from MARDEF loans to start and run small businesses.

Some households (20%) from the treatment group revealed that they were unable to start or run businesses because they had diverted the credit money from MARDEF to buy maize due to the fact that their food stocks had run out.

Only fifteen households from the treatment group stated that they used their income from various sources to repay MARDEF loans. This finding confirms the low loan repayment rate reported by MARDEF from borrowers from Blantyre rural.

4.5   IMPACT OF MARDEF LOANS ON FOOD SECURITY LEVELS OF HOUSEHOLDS IN THE TREATMENT GROUP

The study found no evidence that access to microcredit had a positive impact on improving the food situation of receiving households. Table 13 shows that the majority of households in both the treatment group (88%) and the control group (90%) reported that they had been eating less (usually one meal a day).

Table 13: Number of Meals per Day Taken by Respondents.

Number of Meals per Day	Treatment Group	Control Group
	% of Households involved	% of Households involved
More than 2 meals	2	3
2 meals	10	7
1 meal	88	90
TOTAL	100	100

Source: Research Findings

Furthermore, the interviewed households revealed that they were getting rid of assets (usually livestock) and diverting resources, including MARDEF loans, from production uses to buying food. Looking for casual work (*ganyu*) and food was a daily task preoccupying much productive time of interviewed households in the treatment group. The continuous search for food overrode the time for starting and running small businesses such that most households appeared to be backsliding in their wealth status.

4.6 IMPACT OF MARDEF LOANS ON EDUCATION AND HEALTH SERVICES EXPENDITURE OF HOUSEHOLDS IN THE TREATMENT GROUP

The study found no evidence that access to microcredit helped the beneficiary households in the treatment group to increase their expenditure on education and health services. On the contrary, the results of the study presented in Table 14 and Figure 2 show that spending on education and health services declined sharply between 2004 to 2007 for the interviewed households in both the treatment group and the control group.

Table14: Treatment Group's Expenditure on
Education and Health Services

Year	Income (MK)	Educational Expenditure (MK)
2004	2,410	457
2005	2,321	417.78
2006	2,510	376
2007	2,451	245

Source: Research Findings

Figure2: Treatment Group's Expenditure on Education and Health Services

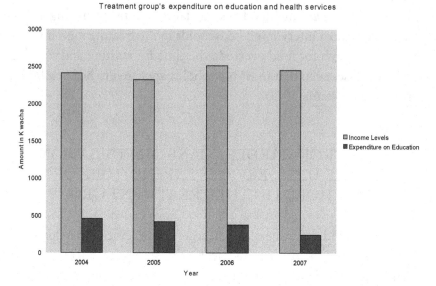

Source: Research Findings

The spending reduction in the period 2004-2007 as shown in Table 14 were probably due to the downturn in the economy or the increased availability of free primary education and free health services provided by the current government of Malawi.

DISCUSSION

The results of the data analysis presented above provide many insights as follows:

1. Microcredit provided by MARDEF to the treatment group does not appear to make a significant contribution to households' accumulation of fixed assets and poverty alleviation as one might expect.

2. Land shortages and small land holding of households is still a major constraint to asset ownership levels and production

levels. The availability of MARDEF loans to some households (treatment group) has not solved this problem. Almost all the households interviewed reported lack of land and small land holding sizes as the main constraint to improvement in their economic and social welfare.

3.   Unlike microcredit, *ganyu*, beer-brewing, and firewood sales appear to make a high contribution to household economic and social welfare. The majority of households spend their income on buying maize for food instead of starting and running businesses.

4.   Some households are diverting part of their MARDEF loans to purchasing maize for food rather than starting and running businesses as expected.

5.   Most importantly, the maximum loan limits (MK10,000.00 or US 70.00 per person) provided by MARDEF are inadequate for poor households to run viable business that can generate enough income to buy physical assets and meet other social needs of households. This is because the cost of operating businesses has increased due to rising transport costs and inflation.

CHAPTER 5

CONCLUSIONS AND RECOMMENDATIONS

5.1 INTRODUCTION

Generally, the results of the study have shown that in the context of Malawi, microcredit appears to make no positive impact on reducing the poverty status of the receiving households. Therefore, the Null hypothesis has not been substantiated and is therefore rejected. Instead, the Alternative hypothesis is accepted and adopted. This means that the general broad research question has been answered negatively.

5.2 CONCLUSIONS

Having analysed and discussed the findings of the study, some conclusions and recommendations are hereby made.

Impact of Microcredit on Accumulation Levels of Fixed Assets

Specifically, the study has found no evidence that access to microcredit had an impact on accumulation levels of fixed assets by receiving households. In fact, the interviewed households in both the treatment group and the control group reported possession of almost similar assets in type, quantity, and value. The respondents in the treatment group explained that the maximum loan of K10,000.00 or US $70.00 per person which they receive from MARDEF was too little for them to acquire additional fixed assets.

Impact of Microcredit on Households' Income Levels

As might be expected, access to microcredit translated into higher income levels for the receiving households in the treatment group than those in the control group. Nevertheless, the results of statistical test (t-test) revealed that the difference in income levels between the treatment group and the control group was not statistically significant. This means that microcredit had no impact on increasing the income levels of the interviewed households in the treatment group and hence no impact on reducing their poverty.

Impact of Microcredit on Production Levels

Microcredit also appeared to have no impact on production levels. Results of the study showed that production levels between the interviewed households from both treatment group and control group did not appear to be significantly different. This was despite the fact that households in the treatment group were benefiting from microcredit provided by MARDEF while households in the control group did not get credit assistance from any institution. The similarities in production levels between the treatment group and the control group can probably be attributed to facing same production constraints, such as the difficult economic conditions due to drought and increases in fertilizer prices and other inputs.

Impact of Microcredit on Food Security Levels

The study found no evidence that access to microcredit had a positive impact on improving the food situation of receiving households. In both groups, the majority of households reported eating less (usually one meal a day), getting rid of assets (usually livestock), and diverting resources, including MARDEF loans, from production uses to buying food. Looking for casual work (ganyu) and food was a daily task preoccupying much productive time of interviewed households in the treatment group. The continuous search for food overrode the time for starting and running small businesses such that most households appeared to be backsliding in their wealth status.

Misconceptions about Government Funded Microcredit Programs

The study has also found that the majority of poor households in rural Malawi had misconceptions about Malawi's government-funded microcredit programs, such as the MARDEF loan scheme. For example, over 75% of the interviewed households in both the treatment group and the control group believed that MARDEF loans are "political campaign money" which they are entitled to receive without any need to pay it back in order to vote the present government back into office during the election period in 2009.

Impact of Microcredit on Expenditure on Education and Health Services

Finally, the study has found no evidence that access to microcredit helped the beneficiary households in the treatment group to increase their expenditure on education and health services. On the contrary, the results of the study have shown that spending on education and health services declined sharply between 2004 to 2007 for the interviewed households in both the treatment group and the control group. The spending reductions were probably related to the downturn in the economy or the increased availability of free primary education and free health services provided by the current government of Malawi.

5.3   RECOMMENDATIONS

From the results of the study, the following actions are recommended to the government of Malawi, MARDEF, and other stakeholders to address the grey areas that inhibit the effectiveness of microcredit to reduce poverty in the rural Malawi.

1.   There is a need that MARDEF should increase the amount of credit disbursed to poor households to enable them run viable business which can generate enough income in sustainable ways to reduce their poverty. The study has revealed that

MARDEF loan beneficiaries do not get adequate loan amounts to run their business activities in a profitable way in the face of escalating transport and other operating costs.

2. To improve the availability of resources and the effectiveness of its microcredit scheme to poor households, MARDEF should identify priority poverty groups (e.g., poultry and vegetable growers) in selected constituencies and develop targeted programs that specifically address the poverty problems of loan beneficiaries in the selected groups. Presently, MARDEF lacks focus because it tries to provide microcredit to all types of businesses in every constituency of Malawi at the same time. This approach requires massive resources, which are just simply not available.

3. Because the statistical results of the study showed that many households in the treatment group and control group had a low level of knowledge and misconceptions about the objectives of MAERDEF microcredit scheme, there is a need to embark on civic education. Nationwide campaigns should be conducted aimed at promoting awareness of the objectives of microcredit programs, especially government-funded microcredit schemes such as MARDEF. The present thinking among most loan beneficiaries, that MARDEF loans are political campaign money that will not be paid back and can be used unproductively, should be discouraged.

4. To improve business success, it is recommended that microcredit should be targeted at the right people with business culture and entrepreneurship spirit. The identified microcredit beneficiaries should be provided with adequate education and training to improve their business management, technical, and leadership skills. The results of the study have revealed that credit groups are formed too quickly and money is also disbursed too quickly, before assessing the group dynamics and entrepreneurship of receiving households. Furthermore, the two-day training provided by MARDEF before extending microcredit to households is reported to be inadequate, bearing

in mind that the majority of receiving households are illiterate and slow in absorbing knowledge due to old age.

5. Apart from insufficient amounts of microcredit, the study has revealed a lot of factors which are inhibiting growth in crop production levels of poor households. Since constraints to production levels are multi-faceted, interventions will be most effective if other components apart from provision of microcredit are also included. For instance, improving access to fertilizer, pesticides, and planting seeds and using non-credit methods can improve production levels and reduce food insecurity and poverty. As many households are used to *"ganyu"*, it is recommended that the government of Malawi should introduce inputs for work (*ganyu*) programs to assist poor households improve production levels in the face of high fertilizer prices and the absence of subsidies for inputs.

6. Livestock can be an asset to sell to buy food during food shortages and to buy medical drugs and pay educational fees for children. However, the majority of the poor households interviewed in both the treatment group and the control group reported not owning livestock, and many had lost animals to diseases. It is therefore recommended that, in addition to the provision of microcredit, separate programs to increase ownership of livestock and improve management should be initiated. This is more imperative and urgent for poor households in Blantyre District rural who are living on the edge of poverty.

7. To increase or maximize the impact of microcredit programs on the alleviation of poverty in receiving households, it is necessary to enhance the cross-sectional collaboration of microcredit institutions operating in rural Malawi. During the study, it was noted that the rural economy in Malawi is served by many microcredit institutions, such as PMERW, MFF, MUSCO, FINCA, PRIDE, MARDEF, etc., which provide microcredit targeted at improving the income levels of poor households. However, each microcredit institution plans and

operates in isolation of others, despite targeting the same poor households. As a result, the study noted that some households were receiving microcredit from two or more institutions, and this is creating problems in loan repayments and monitoring the performance of each credit program.

5.4 RESEARCH LIMITATIONS AND POSSIBLE AREAS OF EXTENTION

The reader notices that the study focused on only one district in the southern region of Malawi (Blantyre district) out of twenty-eight districts of the country benefiting from the five-billion kwacha MARDEF loan scheme. It would be naïve to claim that the results are a true representation of the information on the ground in other districts. So there is need for further research on the impact on microcredit on poverty alleviation of receiving households in other districts in order to get a better picture.

Furthermore, lack of accurate accounting records by respondents made it difficult for the researcher to collect accurate data. The researcher had to rely on oral and recalled information provided by respondents. In many cases it was difficult to verify business transactions in terms of accumulation levels of fixed assets, income levels, production levels, business sales, profits, savings, liabilities, and expenditure levels on education and social services. More research is therefore needed to come up with better ways of measuring movement of poverty alleviation variables.

5.5 BIBLIOGRAPHY

Chinyanga, C. (2007). Unpublished Pamphlet on Research Methods and Statistics, Eastern and Southern African Management Institute (ESAMI), Arusha, Tanzania, May 2007.

Coleman, B. (1999). "The Impact of Group Lending in Northern Thailand." *Journal of Development Economics*, retrieved on 4 March 19 2008 from http:www.elsevier.com/locate/econbase.

Coleman, B (2006). "Microfinance in Northeast Thailand: Who Benefits and How Much?" *World Development Journal*, Vol 34, No. 9, retrieved on 4 March 2008 from www/elsevier.com/locate/world dev.

Cooper, D.R. & Schindler, P. (1998). *Business Research Methods— International Edition.* (6th ed.). Singapore: McGraw-Hill.

David Hulme (1990). "The Limits of Microcredit as a Rural Development Intervention," retrieved on 6 March 2008 from www. gdrc.org.

Diagne and Zeller (2001). *Access to Credit and Its Impact: Net Crop Income as a Measure of Welfare in Malawi.* Research Report 116, International Food Policy Research Institute, Washington, DC.

DFID (2001). *The Impact of Training on Women's Micro-Enterprise: Four Programmes (Ethiopia, India, Peru and Sudan)* supported by ACORD and international technology two UK based NGO.

Elizabeth Dunn(2001). *The Impact of Microcredit: A Case Study from Peru*, University of Missouri, Columbia.

Eswarah and Kotwal (1997). "Implications of Credit Constraints for Risk Behaviour in Less Developed Economies," Oxford Economic Papers N.S. 42.

Government of Malawi (2005). *Situation Analysis of Poverty in Malawi,* Lilongwe, UNICEF.

Gina Neff (1996). *Microcredit: World Business Council For Sustainable Development,* retrieved on 13 December 2007 from gina.wbcsd. org.

IFAD (1998, July). "Ghana—lending for women's income—generating activities, office of evaluation studies; land conversation and smallholder rehabilitation project." *Midterm Evaluation Report.* http://www.gdrc.org/icm/wind/uis-wind.html.

IFAD (2000). "Rural financial services project. Pre-appraisal poverty gender and rural informal sector perspective and working paper: Strategy for mainstreaming gender with specific focus on Northern Ghana," retrieved June 12 2008 from http://www.ifad.org/gender/ learning/finance/sector/finance/43.html.

Karen Mre (1990) "Training and Support of Families on Microcredit," retrieved on 14 December 2007 from http://www.relief web/ library/UNICEF.

Khandkar, M. (2001). "The impact assessment of micro-finance: The psychological dimensions of women's empowerment," *Social Science Review,* 18,(1). Published research paper, Faculty of Social Science, University of Dhaka, Bangladesh.

Khandkar, M. (2003). "Women empowerment in Bangladesh: Credit is not a panacea." Published research paper, Department of Marketing, University of Dhaka. http://www.oneworldaction.org/download/ microfinpps/Khondkararticle.doc.

Lucey T. (1996). *Quantitative Techniques,* Continuum Press Ltd, Condor.

Malawi Government(2001). *Strategies for enhancing the growth of micro, small and medium scale enterprises in Malawi.* Zomba: Government Printing Office.

Malawi Rural Development Fund (2005). *MARDEF Operational Manual, Lilongwe*

Malawi Rural Development Fund (2005). *Inaugural Speech by the State President of the Republic of Malawi,* His Excellency, The State Doctor Bingu Wa Mutharika. Blantyre.

Malawi Government (1999). *Microfinance policy and action plan.* Ministry of Commerce and Industry. Draft.

Malawi Government (2004). *Poverty Alleviation Strategy Paper,* Government Printing Office, Zomba.

Mayoux, L. (1997). "The magic ingredient? Microfinance's empowerment," A briefing paper presented for the microcredit summit, Washington, USA. http://www.gdrc.org/icm/wind/magic.html.

Mayoux, L. & Simanowitz, A. (1999). *Participatory monitoring for poverty reduction and women's empowerment.* South Africa: Small Enterprise Foundation.

Mayoux, L. (2000). "Credit and Savings programme in Cam Xuyen District, Ha Tinth in Vietnam," Published research paper, Save the Children Fund, UK.

Meade J (2001). "An examination of the microcredit movement," retrieved June 22 2008 from http:www.geocities.com/jasonmeade3000/Microcredit.html.

Microcredit Summit Report (1997). Washington DC, Results Education Fund.

Mohammed Yanus (1990). "Creating A World Without Poverty," retrieved on 14 December 2007 from http://www.grameen.infor.org.

New York Times (February 16 1997). "Micro loans for the very poor."

Saunders, M., Phillip, L., & Achian, T. (2000). *Research methods for business students.* Ashford Colour Press Ltd: London.

Still, L.V. (1998). "Women in small business: Towards a new paradigm," Published research paper. University of Western Australia and Wendy Timms Curtin, University of Technology, retrieved June 23 2008 from http://www.sbaer.uca.edu/Research/JCSB/aa003.html.

The Economist (February 27 1993). "Banking on the Poor."

United Nations (2005). "World Summit for Social Development," Copenhagen, UN http://www.un.org/documents.

World Bank (1990). "Malawi: Growth Through Poverty Reduction," Washington DC: World Bank.

World Bank (2001). "2001 World Bank policy research report. Engendering development through gender equality in rights, resources and voice," Oxford University Press.

Zeller and Sharma (1999). "Rural Finance and Poverty Alleviation," Food Policy Report, Washington DC: International Food Policy Research Institute.

APPENDIX 1

AVERAGE MARKET PRICE OF COMMON ASSETS OWNED BY TARGET GROUPS IN THREE CONSTITUENCIES OF BLANTYRE DISTRICT RURAL

TYPE OF ASSET	QUANTITY	MARKET (MKT) PRICES IN KWACHA			AVERAGE PRICE
		MKT 1	MKT 2	MKT 3	
PARCEL OF LAND	< 0.5 ha	20,000	25,000	20,000	21,667
(hectares)	0.5 < 1.0 ha	2,500	30,000	40,000	31,667
	1.0 < 1.5 ha	30,000	40,000	50,000	40,000
	1.5 < 2.0 ha	40,000	45,000	60,000	48,333
PRODUCTIVE ASSETS					
Bicycle	I bicycle	4,500	4,000	4,500	4,333
Hoes	1 hoe	200	250	250	233
Pangas	1 panga	150	150	150	150
Business building (one room)	Rent/month	500	600	600	566
NON-PRODUCTIVE ASSETS					
Dwelling house (one room)	Rent/month	500	700	600	600
	1 bed	600	500	500	533
Furniture	1 chair	400	500	450	450
	1 plate	100	150	120	123
Utensils	1 pot	200	200	200	200
	1 pail	600	650	600	616
LIVESTOCK					
Cattle	1 cow/bull	100,000	100,000	100,000	100,000
Goats (average size)	1 goat	3,000	2,500	3,500	3,000
Pigs (average size)	1 pig	1,000	1,200	1,200	1,133
Chickens (average size)	1 chicken	700	700	700	700
Ducks (average size)	1duck	500	500	500	500
Pigeons (average size)	1 pigeon	250	300	250	266

Source:—Research Findings.

Note: Average prices are based on data collected from three rural markets covered by the research projects in Blantyre District rural.

APPENDIX 2

ESAMI EXECUTIVE MBA DEGREE PROGRAMME RESEARCH QUESTIONNAIRE.

Research Topic: Does Microcredit Really Help in Poverty Alleviation of Its Beneficiaries in Blantyre District of Malawi: The Case of Malawi Rural Development Fund (The 5 Billion Kwacha Loan Scheme)

INTRODUCTION

The researcher is a student pursuing the Master's degree course offered by the Eastern and Southern Africa Management Institute (ESAMI).

The last part of the MBA programme requires the student to conduct an academic research in any module studied, in any area of his interest. This student's topic of study is "The Impact of Microcredit on Poverty Alleviation of the Beneficiaries in Blantyre District of Malawi: The Case of Malawi Rural Development Fund (The 5 Billion Kwacha Loan Scheme)."

You have been selected as a respondent in the research for data collection purposes. Please be assured that this is an academic exercise and all the information that will be collected shall only be used for academic purposes and will be treated with utmost confidentiality.

A. IDENTITY OF RESPONDENT:

Tick

(1) MARDEF Loan Beneficiary
(2) Non-MARDEF Loan Beneficiary

A1	Date of the Interview	
A2	Name of the Enumerator	
A3	Name of the Respondent	

B. DEMOGRAPHIC CHARACTERISTICS OF RESPONDENTS

B1	Age of the Respondent	
B2	Highest qualification of the Respondent	
B3	Occupation of the Respondent • Farming • Household work • Wage labourer • Trader • Other self-employment • Student • Unemployed • Other	State First Occupation ☐ Second Occupation ☐ Third Occupation ☐

C. BUSINESS INFORMATION

C1	How long have you been in business?	Tick Less than one year ☐ Between 1-4 years ☐ Between 5-9 years ☐ 10 years and over ☐
C2	Nature of business(es)	
C3	Date business started	
C4	How much was the starting capital?	K . . . .
C5	What were the sources of capital?	MARDEF loan ☐ Others ☐
C6	What is the target market?	
C7	Number of employees (including owner)	

D. MARDEF AS A MICROCREDIT PROVIDER

D1	When did you first get into contact with MARDEF?	
D2	In what way(s) did you think MARDEF could assist in your business?	
D3	What service(s) did MARDEF provide you?	Tick Loan ☐ Training ☐ Both ☐
D4	If loan, how many times has MARDEF provided you with loan?	
D5	State amounts of loan and the dates	Amount (K) Date K . . . . K . . . . K . . . .
D6	Were you provided with the amounts of loans that you expected?	Yes ☐ No ☐
D7	Did you invest the whole amounts of the loan or not?	Yes ☐ No ☐
D8	What other household needs did you buy or meet with the loan?	
D9	If training, what type of training did you get from MARDEF?	
D10	Did you get the appropriate training suitable for your nature of business?	Yes ☐ No ☐
D11	In what other areas do you need extra training?	

E. IMPACT OF MARDEF CREDIT ON BUSINESS PERFORMANCE

	How has the loan from MARDEF, assisted you in the business		Grown (5)	Stagnated (3)	Declined (1)
E1		Customers			
		Orders			
		Number of business outlets			
		Sales turnover			
E2	How many other businesses did you start due to MARDEF's loan or training programs				
E3	Have you been able to repay any loan borrowed in time?		Yes ☐ No ☐		
E4	If yes, were you paying in part or in full?		In part ☐ In full ☐		
E5	Tick limiting factors in order of seriousness in the operation of your business in descending order; 1 most serious 2 serious and 3 less serious		Most serious (1)	Serious (2)	Less serious (3)
		Access to loan Lack of appropriate training			
		Inadequate demand for goods			
		Lack of technology			

		Lack of business management skills			
		Lack of transport			
E6	Do you wish to continue borrowing from MARDEF after successfully competing repaying the loan?	Yes ▭ No ▭			
E7	If no, tick reasons to your answer in order of importance in descending order; 1 most important, 2 important and 3 less important		Very Important (1)	Important (2)	Less Important (3)
		Interest rate			
		Repayment period too short			
		Insufficient funds			
		Low profits			
E8	What factors contribute to success in your business				
E9	What factors contributed to failure in your business?				

F. ECONOMIC AND SOCIAL WELFARE INFORMATION FOR MEASURING IMPACT OF MARDEF LOANS ON POVERTY ALLEVIATION

POVERTY ALLEVIATION MEASURING VARIABLE	BEFORE RECEIVING MARDEF LOANS	AFTER RECEIVING MARDEF LOANS
ASSET OWNERSHIP AND COMPOSITION		

TYPE OF ASSET OWNED (Value in Malawi Kwacha)		
• All assets	K	K
• Land	K	K
• Productive assets (buildings, equipment)	K	K
• Non-production assets (furniture, utensils)	K	K
• Livestock (cattle, goats, chicken)	K	K
• Other assets	K	K
INCOME LEVELS PER ANNUM SOURCE OF INCOME		
• Crop sales	K	K
• Livestock sales	K	K
• Self-employment	K	K
• Wage employment	K	K
• Business Sales	K	K
• Credit	K	K
• Other sources		
SAVINGS AND INVESTMENTS PER ANNUM		
• Cash savings	K	K
• Assets investments/ bought	K	K

LIABILITIES/DEBT STATUS **TYPE OF DEBT**		
• Household internal borrowing	K	K
• MARDEF debt	K	K
• Debt from banks/ microcredit institutions	K	K
• Debt from other lenders	K	K
PRODUCTION LEVELS PER ANNUM (Measured in Malawi kwacha)		
• Crop production for sales	K	K
• Crop production for consumption	K	K
• Animal production for sales	K	K
• Animal production for consumption	K	K
• Business production	K	K
EXPENSES (in Malawi Kwacha)		
• Household expenses	K	K
• Crop production for consumption	K	K
• Animal production for consumption	K	K
• Business production	K	K

ACCESS TO EDUCATION		
• School expenses for children in households	K	K
• Training expenses for self and spouse	K	K
• School expense for relatives	K	K
ACCESS TO HEALTH CARE		
• Medical expenses for self	K	K
• Medical expenses made for children	K	K
• Medical expenses made for other household members	K	K
FOOD SECURITY		
• Meals per day (average)	K	K
EMPLOYMENT LEVELS		
• Household labourers including owner	K	K
• Other external labourers	K	K

ALL INFORMATION IN THIS QUESTIONNAIRE IS PRIVATE AND CONFIDENTIAL. THANKS FOR YOUR TIME AND CONTRIBUTION.

APPENDIX 3

LIST OF MARDEF OFFICIALS CONSULTED DURING THE STUDY

NAME OF OFFICIAL	DESIGNATION	DATE INTERVIEWD
Mr Alex Mtengula	Operations Manager	22 July 2008
Mr John Nyirenda	Public Relations Officer	23 July 2008
Mr Davie Mutha	Project Officer-Blantyre district	23 July 2008

APPENDIX 4

TREATMENT GROUP_—
LIST OF MARDEF LOAN BENEFICIARIES
INTERVIEWED DURING THE STUDY

	RESPONDENTS	SEX	NAME OF BUSINESS GROUP	AREA
1	Mr Gumbo	Male	Zamunthaka Youth	Blantyre central
2	Mr S. Chikozola	Male	Sakala Youth	Blantyre Central
3	Mr S. Mkandawire	Male	Tikondane	Blantyre Central
4	Mr Chikondi	Male	Tisasalane	Blantyre Central
5	Ms I.T. Ng'oma	Female	Tithandizane disability	Blantyre Central
6.	Ms M. Nkhoma	Female	Kabuthu disability	Blantyre Central
7	Ms Laban	Female	Kupita Business	Blantyre Central
8	Mr P. Jere	Male	Chilungamo	Blantyre Malabada
9	Mr R.G. Demba	Male	Nkhumbe Farming	Blantyre Malabada
10	Mr Chaponda	Male	Tiyese Farming	Blantyre Malabada
11	Mr F. Nyundo	Male	Macheka	Blantyre Malabada
12	Ernest Kasambwe	Male	Tiyanjane	Blantyre Malabada
13	Mr Kawonga	Male	Ulemu tinsmith	Blantyre Malabada
14	Mr Chirwa	Male	Tithokoze	Blantyre Malabada
15	Mr Nyirenda	Male	Tiyamike Mpemba	Blantyre South
16	Ms Kaferawanthu	Female	Chigwirizano Investment	Blantyre South
17	Mr Samson	Male	Chipwete	Blantyre South
18	Edith Mkandawire	Female	Maziko business	Blantyre South
19	Cecilia Mkwanda	Female	Mitomoni	Blantyre South
20	Julie Apha Manda	Female	Kandodo	Blantyre South
21	Rachel Dzanja	Female	Zikhale chakana	Blantyre South
22	Mable Dzanja	Female	Ubale Club	Blantyre East

23	Mercy Kapachika	Female	Khamalipindila	Blantyre East
24	Janet Msowoya	Female	Makasu area	Blantyre East
25	Yvonne Chibambo	Female	Mlombozi area	Blantyre East
26	Jacqueline Sekeni	Female	Mlombozi cotton	Blantyre East
27	Tiwonge Kachali	Female	Phindu group	Blantyre East
28	Nellie Minti	Female	Tamandani group	Blantyre East
29	Chikondi T. Msukwa	Female	Akuzike	Blantyre Bangwe
30	Getrude Mkandawire	Female	Good hope advance	Blantyre Bangwe
31	Mirriam Chenembu	Female	Tiyanjane	Blantyre Bangwe
32	Hannah Supply	Female	Chiasangalalo	Blantyre Bangwe
33	Salah Malekano	Female	Chiyembekezo	Blantyre Bangwe
34	Ellah Paul	Female	Ndirande support	Blantyre South East
35	Esmie Tindo	Female	Tiyanjane group 4	Blantyre South East
36	Chifundo Shackirah Alie	Female	Pafex group	Blantyre South East
37	Steve Mwanyongo	Female	Glory of God	Blantyre South East
38	Innocent Mabutao	Male	Chiyanjano	Blantyre South East
39	Ozuya Longwe	Male	Mlambe	Blantyre South East
40	Lucky Banda	Male	Lucky business	Blantyre South East
41	Dickie Tsakama	Male	Nthochi	Blantyre South West
42	Alfred Kadri Tawakali	Male	Amakwaniritsa	Blantyre South West

APPENDIX 5

CONTROL GROUP—A LIST OF NON-BENEFICIARIES OF MARDEF LOANS INTERVIEWED DURING THE STUDY

	RESPONDENTS	SEX	NAME OF BUSINESS	AREA
1	Ellard Chitalo	Male	Chitawira	Blantyre rural central
2	Ignasio Pondani	Male	Chilobwe	Blantyre rural central
3	Janat Msowoya	Female	Mpagaja	Blantyre rural central
4	Yvonne Chibambo	Female	Bt. Police	Blantyre rural central
5	Jacqueline Sekeni	Female	Chakana	Blantyre rural central
6	Tiwonge Kachali	Female	Mlanga	Blantyre rural central
7	Herbert Phiri	Male	Nthocha	Blantyre rural central
8	Patrick Mphepo	Male	Kampala	Blantyre rural Malabala
9	Alfred Kadri Tawakali	Male	Chakana	Blantyre rural Malabada
10	Charles Lubani	Male	Gamulani	Blantyre rural Malabada
11	Dickie Tsakama	Male	Makata	Blantyre rural Malabada
12	Innocent V. Mabutao	Male	Chatha	Blantyre rural Malabada
13	Hussain Lambat	Male	Msusa	Blantyre rural Malabada
14	Mzanga M Billy	Male	Zingwangwa	Blantyre rural south
15	Ozisa Longwe	Male	Manazse	Blantyre rural south
16	Steve Mwandondo	Male	Naotcha	Blantyre rural south
17	Mr Buleya	Male	Buleya	Blantyre rural south
18	Sub T/A Mduwa	Female	Chilobwe	Blantyre rural south
19	Mrs E.N. Kayuni	Female	Zingwangwa	Blantyre rural south

20	Mr J.P. Sangwa	Male	Manja	Blantyre rural east
21	Mrs Gumbo	Female	Kajombo	Blantyre rural east
22	Mrs Liwonde	Female	Chinupule	Blantyre rural east
23	Mrs Magalanga	Female	Mwalija	Blantyre rural east
24	Mr Bimpi	Male	Mwamadi	Blantyre rural east
25	Mrs Chimodzi	Female	Wisiki	Blantyre rural east
26	Mr Kaulembe	Male	Nkhukuteni	Blantyre rural Bangwe
27	Mr Mbowela	Male	Chiwembe	Blantyre rural Bangwe
28	Mrs Mloyeni	Female	Mondiwa	Blantyre rural Bangwe
29	Mrs Mlonyeni	Female	Chiwembe	Blantyre rural Bangwe
30	Mrs Phiri	Female	Manjombe	Blantyre rural Bangwe
31	Mrs Phiri	Female	Chiswe	Blantyre rural Bangwe
32	Mrs Kalawe	Female	Misesa	Blantyre rural Bangwe
33	Mr Nkhoma	Male	Chemboma	Blantyre rural south east
34	Mrs Zimba	Female	Anderson	Blantyre rural south east
35	Ms Hara	Female	Manyowe	Blantyre rural south east
36	Ms Hara	Female	Chemusa	Blantyre rural south east
37	Mr Chikozolo	Male	Likotima	Blantyre rural south east
38	Ms M. Nkhoma	Female	Lupugama	Blantyre rural south east
39	Mr S. Mkandawire	Male	Kumanda	Blantyre rural north
40	Mrs Nyundo	Female	Lemu	Blantyre rural north
41	Mrs Samson	Female	Singano	Blantyre rural north
42	Mr M. Gere	Male	Peturo	Blantyre rural north

Sample MBA Thesis—
The Survey Research Design
(Qualitative Approach)

Note: Names marked with a * are fictitious in the sample thesis.

THE DIRECT ECONOMIC IMPACT
OF THE OPERATIONS OF THE
INTERNATIONAL CRIMINAL TRIBUNAL
FOR RWANDA ON ARUSHA

by

Gloria Maxwell*

This paper was submitted in partial fulfilment of the requirements for the award of ESAMI/MsM Degree of Master's of Business Administration.

EASTERN AND SOUTHERN
AFRICAN MANAGEMENT INSTITUTE
P. O. BOX 3030
ARUSHA
TANZANIA

To my Children, Peter*, Joyce*, and Paul*

To my beloved Charles*,

To my Mother and to the happy memory of my Father

ACKNOWLEDGEMENTS

For the development and production of this work, I feel a deep sense of gratitude:

- To my supervisor, Professor Ben Michael* for his guidance and supervision.
- To the ESAMI and MsM Faculties and Consultants for sharing their knowledge and expertise with me throughout the Executive MBA Curriculum.
- To Professor John Moses* for his availability and willingness to assist.
- To the International Criminal Tribunal for Rwanda (ICTR) for the multidimensional support extended to me. I am particularly grateful to Assistant Secretary General, Registrar of the ICTR for granting me the authorization to access his organization's information. My thanks go to those staff who were kind enough to respond to the survey, who imparted some valuable information to the research or shared their valuable time, expertise, or experience with me.
- To all my friends and MBA colleagues for their support throughout this demanding journey—the MBA years.

My profound gratitude to all the other people not mentioned here, who in one way or the other assisted me in completing this research paper and the Executive MBA program in whole.

CONTENTS

LIST OF TABLES

LIST OF FIGURES

LIST OF ABBREVIATIONS

ACABQ — Advisory Committee on Administrative and Budgetary Questions

AICC — Arusha International Conference Centre

DSA — Daily Subsistence Allowance

EAC — East African Community

ESAMI — Eastern and Southern African Management Institute

GDP — Gross Domestic Product

ICTR — International Criminal Tribunal for Rwanda

MIP — Medical Insurance Plan

OPPBA — Office of Program Planning, Budget, and Accounts

PPF — Para-Statal Pension Funds

TSH — Tanzanian Shilling

UN — United Nations

UNDF — United Nations Detention Facility

UNICTR — United Nations International Criminal Tribunal for Rwanda

UNMISET — United Nations Mission of Support in East Timor

USA — United States of America

UNTAC — United Nations Transitional Authority in Cambodia

UNTAET — United Nations Transitional Administration for East Timor

EXECUTIVE SUMMARY

The International Criminal Tribunal for Rwanda (ICTR) is a vital participant in the Arusha community. In addition to providing cultural contact with people from different countries, which enriches the community members as well as the experience and knowledge acquired by National staff, the ICTR has been a major contributor to the economy of Arusha. Its contribution includes the provision of jobs, expenditures on goods and services, and the generation of municipal tax revenues. ICTR also brings in revenues, which would otherwise not be generated in the municipality.

To estimate the economic significance of ICTR, this study measures the tangible benefits of the tribunal in the municipality from January 2002 to December 2004. ICTR expenditures were derived from accounting data obtained from the tribunal. Staff expenditures represented the computation of the net salary paid to the national staff and the portion of their salary paid in Arusha in the case of international staff. The other expenditures used in this study are the stipends paid to legal researchers and the daily subsistence allowance (DSA) paid to the defence teams when working in Arusha. This framework yields direct expenditures for each category of ICTR related expenditures. The multiplier effect of ICTR expenditures was not computed due to the lack of authoritative value of the multiplier.

During the years 2002 to 2004, the ICTR generated $58,796,561 in total economic activity in Arusha through its direct spending on goods and services and the expenditures made by its community.

ICTR's expenditures on goods and services generated $16,161,634 in total economic activity within the area.

ICTR'S legal researchers and defence teams during the same period spent $428,750 in Arusha via the DSA and stipend paid by the tribunal.

The total amount of the local portion of international staff salary assumed to have been spent in Arusha was estimated at $33,093,503. In addition, an estimated amount of $1,920,760 paid by its staff to local educational institutions was disbursed by the ICTR under its education grant program.

ICTR local staff received a total net salary of $6,695,614 during the same period. They also received a contributory health insurance of $422,599 from the tribunal.

According to the information gathered through the survey undertaken in the framework of this research, 1,597 employments were created by international staff and 375 by the national staff working with the tribunal.

The same survey indicates that a monthly amount estimated at $932,890 was spent by international staff on rent, household, utilities, etc., while locally recruited colleagues spent an estimated amount of Tshs 133,915,957 or $117,988 monthly under the same headings.

Figure ES.1: Estimated Direct Impact of ICTR
on the Economy of Arusha

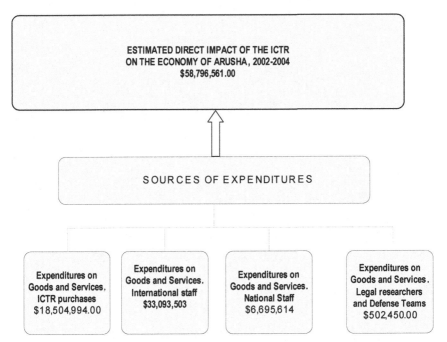

ESTIMATED DIRECT IMPACT OF THE ICTR
ON THE ECONOMY OF ARUSHA, 2002-2004
$58,796,561.00

SOURCES OF EXPENDITURES

Expenditures on
Goods and Services,
ICTR purchases
$18,504,994.00

Expenditures on
Goods and Services,
International staff
$33,093,503

Expenditures on
Goods and Services,
National Staff
$6,695,614

Expenditures on
Goods and Services,
Legal researchers
and Defense Teams
$502,450.00

Source: Author's Estimates

CHAPTER 1

PROBLEM STATEMENT

1.1 INTRODUCTION

After presenting a general background of Arusha and of the International Criminal Tribunal for Rwanda, this chapter focuses on the following substantive topics: statement of the problem situation; research questions and objectives; significance of the study; and conceptual framework. It ends with the structure of the research paper.

1.2 Background

The third largest Tanzanian city (behind Dar es Salaam and Mwanza), Arusha Municipality is the capital of the Arusha region, the largest region of Tanzania (82,428 km²). The municipality covers an area of 93 km². Its population increased from 5,300 people in 1948 to 282,712 in 2002. The growth rate is 4.8% against the national rate or 2.8%[1]. According to the Arusha Municipal Council, the high rate of population influx into the city is due to the fact that to Arusha is a tourist town and the municipality is the main market for minerals and the Mererani mines.

This lovely town is located on the southern slopes of Mount Meru (4,566 meters). It lies between 1,450 and 1,160 meters above sea level.[2] Because of the fertile volcanic soils and the two rainy seasons, agriculture is a major source of income for most inhabitants of Arusha. This traditionally agricultural region is also famous as one of the major

---

[1]   Arusha Municipal Council, Socio-Economic Profile Year 2004, page 1
[2]   *Ibid*, page 1

East African tourist destinations. The liberalization of the mining sector is said to have significantly contributed to the perceived dynamism of the region's economy.

Another distinguishing factor of the city's economic life is the presence of a few regional and/or international organizations, some of which are headquartered in Arusha, such as the Eastern and Southern African Management Institute (ESAMI), the East African Community (EAC), and the United Nations International Criminal Tribunal for Rwanda (UNICTR).

The International Criminal Tribunal for Rwanda (ICTR) was established by the United Nations Security Council Resolution 955 (1994) as a response to serious violations of international humanitarian law committed in Rwanda and neighbouring states, and to the threat they pose to peace and security. The ICTR has authority to prosecute persons responsible for genocide and other serious violations of international humanitarian law committed with the territory of Rwanda between 1 January and 31 December 1994. Its task is then to help restore and maintain peace and bring about national reconciliation. The ICTR also has offices at Kigali (Rwanda), The Hague (The Netherlands) and New York (USA). It consists of three organs, namely, the chambers, the prosecution, and the registry.

The chambers are composed of judges elected by the General Assembly of the United Nations. The judges are expected to be persons of high moral character, impartiality and integrity who possess the qualifications required in their respective countries for appointment to the highest judicial offices.[3] They are responsible for adjudicating cases brought before them at the trial and appellate levels. The judges elect from amongst themselves a president who is in charge of presiding over all the plenary meetings of the tribunal, coordinating the work of

---

[3] See article 12 of the ICTR Statute published as an appendix to UN Security Council Resolution 955(1994) adopted on 8 November 1994

the chambers, supervising the activities of the registry, and exercising any other functions conferred on him by the statute and the rules of procedure and evidence. The chambers are comprised of three trial chambers (ordinarily sitting in Arusha) and an appeals chamber (shared with the International Criminal Tribunal for the former Yugoslavia based at The Hague in The Netherlands). The chambers are composed of sixteen permanent independent judges and a maximum of four *ad litem* independent judges.

The prosecutor is responsible for investigating and prosecuting persons responsible for the crimes falling within the jurisdiction of the ICTR. The office of the prosecutor is subdivided into two main divisions respectively in charge of investigations and prosecutions, with the first one based in Kigali and the second one in Arusha. The investigations division is responsible for tracking those who masterminded the genocide and for gathering evidence of their involvement in the 1994 events. Composed of trial attorneys, the prosecution division is responsible for transforming into indictments the evidence gathered during the investigations and for defending the prosecution cases before the judges of the tribunal.

The Office of the Registrar is headed by a registrar and is responsible for the overall administration and management of the tribunal. It provides judicial, legal, administrative, and logistic support services for the work of the trial chambers, the prosecution, and the defence counsel. The registry also performs other legal functions assigned to it under the tribunal's Rules of Procedure and Evidence and is the tribunal's channel of communication. The registry consists of two divisions respectively in charge of judicial and legal services, and of administrative support services. Operations ran by the registry include the management of the Witnesses and Victims Support Program, the United Nations Detention Facility in Arusha, the ICTR's legal aid program, relations with the host country, etc.

The average annual budget of the ICTR over its ten-year presence in Arusha is $840,809,100.[4] At its headquarters, the organization employs 725 persons, 66.20%[5] of whom are international staff from eighty-five nationalities.

1.3   Statement of the Problem Situation

By its resolution 977 of 22 February 1995[6], the Security Council of the United Nations decided to locate the ICTR in Arusha, in the United Republic of Tanzania.

However, Arusha those days lacked any capacity to host such a tribunal. Within the local community, expectations of the benefits that the presence of the organization could generate, especially with regard to its poor facilities, were high. *Arusha Times* captured the situation as follows: "Arusha, in general, will have its roads improved to international standards. Many run-down tourists' hotels will be refurbished and more money will change hands among businesses and service providers of Arusha."[7] The initial running of the tribunal's activities in Arusha was in fact hampered by this lack of facilities. The United Nations Under-Secretary for Internal Oversight Services is said to have reported that Arusha was not a suitable location for the tribunal because it lacked basic facilities and infrastructure and recommended a search for a more suitable location. *Arusha Times* summarised the situation by this sarcastic headline: "Tribunal finds Arusha Primitive."[8]

---

[4]   formation submitted by the ICTR budget Officer
[5]   Information submitted by the Human Resource and Planning Section of the ICTR
[6]   www.ictr.org
[7]   The Arusha Times, September 1-15, 1995, No. 0001
[8]   The Arusha Times, May 1-15, 1998, N0. 0062

Sometime before this declaration, the same newspaper[9] published that "The proposed Rwanda United Nations Tribunal and the East African Cooperation secretariats to be based here will boost both business and the status of the area." And since the establishment of the ICTR, Arusha has undergone a noticeable economic development.

1.4   Research Questions

Below are some of the questions that have guided the research.

1.   How much economic benefit does the city of Arusha derive by hosting the ICTR?
2.   How much did the ICTR spend in Arusha through its huge operation?
3.   How much does the ICTR staff spend in the form of household expenses in Arusha?
4.   In which sectors can the impact be perceived?

1.5   Research Objectives

This study is intended to make a logical contribution to the understanding of how an institution can provide significant economic benefits to the municipality in which it is established. The study identifies the economic benefits of the ICTR's presence as a functioning organization within the Arusha city. The contribution of the ICTR will be examined in terms of:

1.   The direct monetary benefits to the Arusha business community.
2.   The lessons drawn from such impact.

---

[9]   *Ibid*, September 1-15, 1995. No 0001

1.6   Significance of the Study

The research findings could be useful to various stakeholders, including:

1.   The United Nations takes it for granted that its operations have had a positive impact on the life and economy of Arusha and its environs, but no comprehensive information on the subject exists even within the United Nations. This study could therefore provide the UN with a clearer picture of the impact of its operations on this area. A knowledge of the magnitude of the impact of its closure on Arusha's economy and life would enable the UN to plan its anticipated closure with the interest of the community that has hosted this institution in mind. This study could also help the UN as a whole in its planning of the establishment of future operations similar to the ICTR in comparable contexts.

2.   The Government of Tanzania, Arusha Municipal Council, and interested stakeholders in Arusha could use the findings of this research to work on a strategy aimed at ensuring that Arusha minimizes the losses that may occur due to the departure of ICTR and seize the opportunities that this closure would certainly generate.

3.   Arusha community as a whole could better appreciate the magnitude of the economic role of the ICTR in the life of Arusha and contribute in reshaping the image of this institution in the eyes of the host community.

Finally, this research could provide guidance to other countries where institutions of the likes of the ICTR are to enable them be established to better anticipate the possible impacts on their economic environment and thus maximize the returns on such investments.

1.7   Conceptual Framework of the study

Uma Sekaran defines the conceptual or theoretical framework as "a conceptual model of how one theorizes or makes logical sense of the relationships among the several factors that have been identified as important to the problem."[10]

The basic framework of this study is built around the conceptual model below (see Figure 1).

The International Criminal Tribunal for Rwanda is the organization studied, but what we are interested in researching is its contribution to the local economy of Arusha. The contribution of the ICTR therefore represents the dependent variable that lends itself for investigation.

The variables that influence the dependent variable (contribution of ICTR) are the sectors of the ICTR that have contributed to the local community. These are the direct ICTR expenditures.

The ICTR itself, through its maintenance and operation expenditures, has contributed to the local economy.

The following category of persons also contribute to the local economy: employees who use the income received from the ICTR to purchase goods and services in the local market, defence lawyers who receive a daily subsistence allowance (DSA) which is used to purchase goods and services in the local economy and is paid to them to cover their expenses during their stays in Arusha, and legal researchers who also purchase goods and services in Arusha. There are other independent variables, such as the expenditures of consultants, experts, and visitors, which were not integrated in this framework because of the unavailability of information and time constraints.

---

[10]   Uma Sekaran, *Research Methods for Business, A skill Building Approach*, Fourth edition, 2003; p. 87

At the centre of the expenditures is the ICTR, which purchases goods and services in the local market. Staff and other related workers earn income and DSA and spend in the local market as well. Businesses receive revenues from ICTR and its community and pay their operating costs, and the local government receives taxes from them. The income-spending—income-re-spending cycle constitutes the multiplier process to which reference will be made in further research.

Figure 1.1: Conceptual Framework of the Study

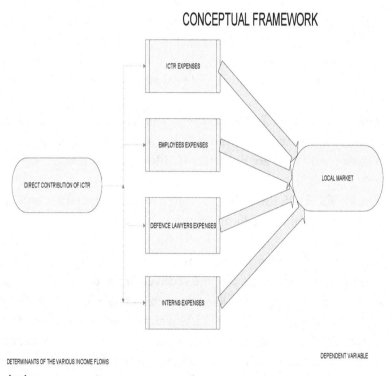

CONCEPTUAL FRAMEWORK

DETERMINANTS OF THE VARIOUS INCOME FLOWS

DEPENDENT VARIABLE

Source: Author

What sets the ICTR apart is that all its revenues are received from sources external to the local economy. In terms of the local economy's circular flow of income and expenditures, ICTR injects external funds into the local community, stimulating more local economic activity than that generated by the re-circulation of local funds by some service providers.

1.8   Structure of the paper

The rest of the paper is organized in four chapters. The second chapter examines existing knowledge on the subject.

The third chapter presents the methodology and procedures used to analyse the problem.

The fourth chapter of the paper presents the findings. It examines the direct contribution of the ICTR via the expenditures made by the organization itself, its employees, legal researchers, and defence teams in the local economy. It also analyses the local and external portions of the tribunal expenditures on goods and services.

Finally, the fifth chapter provides a summary and a conclusion of the study and then outlines a set of general and specific issues to be taken into consideration by the United Nations, the Tanzanian authorities, and other stakeholders.

CHAPTER 2

LITERATURE REVIEW

2.1   Introduction

The total economic impact of an organization is very hard to measure. It may be measured from a short-term or a long-term perspective and calculated in regards to tangible or intangible benefits to the local economy, state, or any defined study area. The intangibles include the private and social benefits, such as the improvement in the quality of life of a community. Both, long-run and intangible benefits are very difficult to measure when compared to tangible benefits.

This chapter begins with the socio-economic profile of Arusha and then examines the literature on economic impact.

2.2   Socio-Economic Profile of Arusha

The economy of Arusha depends on commerce, industry, small-scale agriculture, and tourism. Commercial and industrial activities contribute significantly to the GDP of the municipality.

2.2.1   Industry Sector

Arusha is host to many industries. The main ones are General Tyre East Africa Limited, Tanzania Breweries Ltd, Sunflag, Tanzania Pharmaceutical Industries, etc. There are also about 200 small-scale industries, some of which have closed down because of lack of raw materials, poor management, financial constraints, and stiff competition from imported products.

2.2.2   Commerce and Trade Sector

Commerce and trade is said to be the major occupation of the residents of Arusha. Due to the high influx of people, particularly school leavers, informal sector activities were promoted, such as carpentry, tailoring, shoe-making, etc. These activities have so far managed to employ about 48,725 people, which represents approximately twenty per cent of the municipal residents.[11]

Further, trade liberalization and the limited number of individuals the public establishments can recruit have increased the number of persons involved in trade and commerce.

Table 2.1: Number of Licensed Business Operators in Arusha[12]

Year	No. of Licenses Issued
1996	3,834
1997	2,933
1998	2,274
1999	3,520
2000	4,201
2001	5,519
2002	2,953
2003	3,702

2.2.3   Agriculture and Livestock

In the Arusha municipality, agriculture holds a very important position as a means for foodstuff and cash crop production. About 59,000 people are involved in agricultural activities, which occupy 6,400 hectares of arable land[13]. The crops farmers grow in Arusha municipality are maize,

---

[11]   Ministry of Regional Administration and Local Government, Arusha Municipal Council, Socio-economic profile Year 2004, page 3

[12]   Ibid, page 3

[13]   Ibid, page 4

beans, millet, wheat, chickpeas, fruits, coffee, and other leguminous crops. Small-scale agriculture is still practiced here. People use hand hoes, and very few household use oxen-drawn farm implements like ploughs.

With regard to livestock, a total of 4,000 improved-breed cows are kept under zero grazing in urban wards and produce approximately 48,000 litres of milk per day. Other livestock species, including 20,000 beef cattle, 18,000 goats, and 15,000 other livestock, are kept mainly in wards where traditional livestock keepers live.[14]

2.2.4 Tourism

Arusha is the gateway to the world-famous nationals parks and conservation areas of Tanzania—Mount Kilimanjaro, Arusha National Park, Lake Manyara National Park, Haranguer National Park, Ngorongoro Crater, Olduvai Gorge, and Serengeti National Park. Kilimanjaro is the highest mountain in Africa.

There are eleven tourist hotels in Arusha and eighty-four registered tour operator companies.[15] The tourism industry has created employment opportunities and market outlets for traditional handicraft products.

2.2.5 Health

Health services are found all over the Arusha municipality. However, their concentration is higher in town compared to the rural area. Some of them are under the authority of the Arusha municipality and others under the private sector.

There are five hospitals, one of which belongs to private institutions. There are also seven health centres, forty-five dispensaries, ten

---

[14] Ibid, page 5
[15] Ibid, page 6. Figures are of 2004.

pharmacies, and 146 medical stores. The patient-bed ratio is 279 people per bed in hospitals[16]

The main common diseases affecting residents are malaria, pneumonia, diarrhoea, intestinal worms, AIDS, and skin infections.

2.2.6   Education

In the Arusha municipality, there are 146 schools, including 96 preparatory schools, 36 primary schools, and 14 secondary schools[17]. Most public primary schools are overcrowded. In some schools, for example, there are ninety pupils in a single room instead of the standard number of forty-five. There are twenty-six public primary schools, which can accommodate only 75% of the demand, and the public secondary schools can admit only 560 students for form one per year out of more than 3,800 students who completed their primary school.[18]

2.3   Economic Impact Assessment

2.3.1   What is Economic Impact?

Economic impact studies are useful tools many institutions or organizations utilize to examine their effect within their local and/or regional economies.

Harry Cummings and Don Murray[19] define economic impact as a "measure of the effect of a sector or new project on other sectors of the local economy and the impact can be measured in terms of regional community income; employment; investment; property values;

[16]   Ibid, page 10
[17]   Ibid, page 13
[18]   Ibid, pages 14 & 15
[19]   www.evaluationontario.ca/pdf/Harry   Cummings_CES2002.pdf   A Kinder, Gentler, Simpler Economic Impact Assessment Process.

construction; revenues, expenditures, and capital costs; wages and taxes."

Similarly, Glen Weisbrod and Burton Weisbrod[20] state that economic impacts are effects on the level of economic activity in a given area and that those impacts may be viewed in terms of business output or sales volume, the value-added or gross regional product, wealth including property values, and personal income including wages or jobs. Any of these measures can then be an indicator of improvement in the economic well-being of an area's residents.

According to a study conducted by "UK Sport, Major Sports Events,"[21] economic impact on a host city is the total amount of additional expenditure generated within a city that can be directly or indirectly attributed to the staging of a major event.

2.3.2   How are Economic Impacts Measured?

The economic impacts of a development are almost never contained within the boundaries of a single municipality. If even one employee lives outside the municipality, some of the economic benefits and/or costs will leak beyond the municipal boundaries, and hence not all the benefits of a development will be contained within one municipality. So it is important to estimate the proportion of employment and spending that will occur in the municipality in order to accurately represent what the impact will be.[22]

---

[20]   www.edrgroup.com, Measuring the Economic Impact of Projects and Programs, April 1997, Economic Development Research Group, Boston, MA

[21]   www.uksport.gov.uk, The Economic Impact of Major Events

[22]   www.reddi.mah.gov.on.ca, Economic Impact Assessment

The measures of economic impact are various. According to Glen Weisbrod and Burton Weisbrod[23], there are several measures of economic impacts, and each of them reflects a particular improvement in the local economy.

1. Total employment reflects the number of additional jobs created by economic growth.
2. Aggregate wages and salaries in an area rise as pay levels rise or additional employees are hired.
3. Value added reflects the sum of wage income and corporate profit generated in the study area. It is the equivalent of gross domestic product or gross regional product.
4. Business output includes the full (gross) level of business revenue, which pays for costs of materials and costs of labour, as well as generating net business income (profits).
5. Property values are also a reflection of generated income and wealth.

Weisbrod and Weisbrod indicate that these measures cannot be added together because they are overlapping. For example, a portion of business output (revenue) goes to pay worker's incomes and generates profits, which are also the components of value added.

2.3.3 Some Important Concepts

Direct effects are the initial effects caused by a specific activity, for example, the initial investment in the construction of a building or the effects of the purchase of utilities and supplies and the hiring of local employees, etc.

The direct impacts are defined by Harry Cummings and Don Murray as "the initial, immediate effects caused by a specific activity—i.e. employment and income. Direct impacts initiate subsequent rounds

---

[23] Glen Weisbrod, Burton Weisbrod, Measuring Economic Impacts of Projects and Programs, April 1997.

of income creation, spending and re-spending and result in indirect and induced effects." Daniel J. Stynes[24] defines them as production changes associated with the immediate effects of changes in tourism expenditures. For example, an increase in the number of tourists staying overnight in hotels would directly yield increased sales in the hotel sector.

Indirect effects are those changes to production, employment, incomes, etc., which take place as a result of the direct effects and include the effects on industry that may be directly or indirectly related to the initially impacted sector. Harry Cummings and Don Murray define them as the effects that result from the forward and backward linkages that produce the direct effect. [25] Weisbrod and Weisbrod define them as business growth or decline resulting from changes in the sale of suppliers to the directly-affected business.

Induced effects are the effects of household spending in the regional economy. They arise from a general change in the household sector's earnings and spending patterns and from economic changes due to direct and indirect effects. According to Billy Kinsey Jr,[26] they are the impacts from changes in household expenditures. Similarly, Weisbrod and Weisbrod, define them as further shifts in spending on food, clothing, shelter, and other consumer goods and services as a consequence of change in workers and payroll of directly and indirectly affected businesses. This leads to further business growth or decline throughout the local economy.

Leakages are those expenditures that "leak" out of the country and cannot be included in estimating the economic impact at the local level. For example, when the UNICTR purchases office supplies in the local market, the profits and subsequent employment theoretically stay

---

[24] ; Daniel J. Stynes, Economic Impacts of Tourism
[25] www.reddi.mah.gov.on.ca, Section3: Economic Impact Assessment
[26] www.vcu.edu, Billy Kinsey Jr. The economic Impact of Museums and Cultural Attraction: Another Benefit for the Community

within the region. However, if the office supplies are purchased outside the region, the economic effects are felt in the region from which the supplies were bought. The positive gains cannot be captured locally.

The *multiplier* is an estimate of how much additional economic activity will result from an investment in the economy. It is called "multiplier" because total impacts are larger than the initial, direct impacts. For example, an aggregate economic multiplier of 2.5 would mean that for each dollar spent at an event, $2.50 is generated. Subtracting the original $1.00 spent on the event (direct impact) leaves $1.50 of additional spending on items and services (indirect and induced impact).

2.4   Economic Impacts Studies

Published studies of the economic impact of UN field operations are very rare. A report by the United Nations Transitional Authority in Cambodia's Economic Advisor's Office, titled *The Impact of UNTAC on Cambodia's Economy* (1992)[27] is the only available systematic analysis of the economic impacts of UN missions. However, missions are legally and operationally very different from the ICTR. Missions generally intervene in post-conflict countries and mainly operate within their boundaries. The scope of their mandate is in most cases bigger than that of a specialized institution like the ICTR. Their budget is also huge and the flow of money into the local economy considerable.

The Peace Dividend Trust[28], in association with the United Nations and other partners, is currently undertaking a research on the economic impact of peacekeeping operations. Referring to the situation of the United Nations Transitional Administration for East Timor (UNTAET) and the United Nations Mission of Support in East

---

[27]   UNTAC, 1992, Impact of UNTAC on Cambodia's Economy, Phnom Penh, 1992

[28]   www.peacedividendtrust.org/problemspotential.htm#

Timor (UNMISET)[29], it notes that very little of the budget allocated to the mission is spent in the local economy. Illustrating its statement, it indicates that the multinational mission had a budget of $547 million in 2001, of which $5 million or just 1% was allocated to local labour. During the same period, the entire gross domestic product (GDP) of East Timor was less than $80 million. The resources injected into the local economy were made through local procurement, expenditures of national staff, and the spending of international staff. Due to the shortage of skilled and qualified local labour, the multinational mission recruited the best human resource available on the local market.

Another study by the Economic Adviser's Office of UNTAC[30] assesses the effects of UNTAC's presence in Cambodia. Most of the goods utilized by UNTAC were purchased abroad. Only a small portion of its budget was spent directly. UNTAC's purchasing power nevertheless had considerable direct and indirect employment generating effects. In the seven month period through June 1992, UNTAC supplied jobs to over 800 local staff, paying them a corresponding income of $161,000.

Grant Curtis[31] in his analysis mentioned that the salary of locally hired UNTAC staff was at least fifteen times greater than that of most Cambodians. State sector salaries, in particular, remained very low and were often several months in arrears. The purchasing power of civil service salaries was seriously eroded by the depreciation of the local currency.

---

[29] UNTAET and UNMISET were established to maintain the security of Timor-Leste and build peace.

[30] Impact of UNTAC on Cambodia's Economy, Report prepared by the economic adviser's office, UNTAC, Phnom Penh, Cambodia, December 21 1992

[31] Grant Curtis, *United Nations Research Institute for Social Development, DP 48, Transition to What?*, Cambodia, UNTAC and the peace process, November 1993

Other studies on economic impacts assess the impact of universities on their communities' economy. Ross B. Emmett and Varghese A. Manaloor address the extent to which the flow of income and expenditures in the Camrose area is increased by the presence of the Augustana University.[32] In addition to being a major contributor to the economy of Camrose, the college provides educational services which enrich the quality of community members' lives and enhance their career opportunities. The contribution includes the provision of jobs, the expenditures on locally-provided labour, goods, and services, and the generation of municipal tax revenues. The expenses generated by students, faculties, staff, and administrators were examined. Multipliers were used to estimate the indirect expenditures. Because a high proportion of student spending occurs in the area, the multiplier for students was higher than that for the other forms of direct expenditures covered. It was estimated to be 4.2.

R. Healey and K. Akerblom[33] estimated the direct impact of Queen's University on the Kingston area to be more than $567 million. While most of the Queen's revenues come from outside Kingston, most of the expenditures are made locally through direct expenditures of the university combined with expenditures of faculties, staff, students, and visitors. The university complex has facilitated the establishment of over twenty businesses in the Kingston area, providing several employment opportunities and thereby stimulating the local economy.

---

[32] Ross B. Emmett, Varghese A. Manaloor, *Augustana University College and the Camrose Area. An Economic Impact Study,* May 2000. The University is located in Canada

[33] www.queensu.ca/irp/pdfiles/misc/EconImpSepo3.pdf, *Office of Institutional Research and Planning. Queen's University and the Kingston Area: An Economic Partnership,* September 2003, Report originally published in 1994. Updated by R. Healey and K. Akerblom. The Queen's University is based in Canada

In the Economic Impact of Tarleton State University—Stephenville[34], the impact of the university, its employees, student body, visitors, and the retirees on the local and state economies is measured. The study quantifies the short-run impact of the university and attempts to measure the direct, indirect, and induced impacts of the university. A major portion of the study was conducted using the implant input/ output model. The information collected on expenses made by the university, employees, students, etc., was matched with other data developed for the implant model.

While economic impacts are varied according to the type of organization, project, or mission, they are always considered as a measure of the effect of a sector or new project on other sectors of the local economy. Our study combines some elements of the previous studies by examining the contribution of the UNICTR to the local economy.

---

[34] S. Hussain Ali Jafri; Santhosh K. Durgam; D'Anna a. Jackson, Zeb Pomerenke (2004), *Economic Impact of Tarleton State University—Stephenville*, Stephenville, Texas

CHAPTER 3

RESEARCH METHODOLOGY

3.1   Introduction

This chapter discusses at some length the methodology used to study the contribution of the International Criminal Tribunal of Rwanda to Arusha's economy. It is mainly a descriptive study, and the main instruments used to collect data were interviews and questionnaires. A large amount of data came from the financial report of the ICTR.

3.2   Definition of Study Population

"Population" refers to the entire group of people, events, or things of interest that the researcher wishes to investigate.[35]

For the purpose of this research, our population will be the ICTR staff members, both local and international. This population will allow us to have an idea of the amount of their expenditures in the city of Arusha. This is because our topic is limited to this city.

The ICTR itself is a population. It will provide us data on all their expenses in and out of Arusha, including the data on the number of international and local staff it employs.

The Arusha International Conference Center (AICC) was chosen because it is the landlord of ICTR's headquarters, contained in an office

---

[35]   Uma Sekaran, *op. cit.*

space of 10,000m^2 out of a total of 23,000m^2 office space available in the premises of AICC. [36]

The government officers will give us information on the socio-economic growth of the city and their opinion about the presence of the ICTR.

The business community will also give us their opinion about the presence of ICTR and how it has impacted on their business. The general population is also part of the population.

3.3   Scope of the Study

This study has been limited to the contribution of the International Criminal Tribunal for Rwanda to the economy of Arusha. It will, however, rely only on the variables shown in the conceptual framework, i.e., the expenditures of the ICTR itself, those of its employees, defence councils, and interns. It shall cover the period running from January 2002 through April 2005. All the data were not available on contributions made by the ICTR itself through its operation and maintenance; such as travel tickets bought by the tribunal for its staff for various purposes, travel tickets bought for defence counsel, consultants, experts, legal researchers, etc. Some other expenses, such as the DSA paid to experts, consultants, etc., expenses made by visitors of the ICTR and those made by the visitors of staff, as well as expenses made by some agencies like Hirondelle, Radio France Internationale (RFI), etc., based in Arusha because of the presence of the tribunal were also not covered.

The indirect effects, as well as the induced effect, are beyond the scope of this study. There was no survey about the proportion of the purchases made by the ICTR and its community from various businesses, compared to the total sales they were making. The number of jobs created in these businesses because of the purchasing power of

---

[36]   www.aicc.co.tz/article -profile.htrr, AICC, Corporate Profile

ICTR and its community as well as the expenditures generated by the employees of those businesses. It was also difficult to know the size of the multiplier effect, which is determined by the allocation between savings, imported spending, and local spending. This would have given us an indication of the indirect expenditures generated by ICTR and its community spending.

Finally, the geographical scope of this study was not strictly limited to the administrative boundaries of Arusha city. Arusha was conventionally considered to include, as and when required, the immediate vicinity of the city or its natural extensions. Though administratively not part of Arusha, Kisongo, for example was included because this area is host to all the international schools.

3.4   Justification of the Sample Size and Sample Selection Method

According to the data collected from the Human Resources and Planning Section of the ICTR, the total number of staff members as of August 2005[37] was 725, with 480 international staff and 245 local.

The table of the sample size for a given population size was used.[38] As per this table, the minimum sample size for a population of 700 is 248. The minimum sample size for a population of 750 is 254, and for a population of 850 the minimum sample size should be 265.

In the case of the ICTR headquarters in Arusha, the minimum sample size for a population of 725 will be 251.

A 5% margin of error (which is a measurement of the accuracy of the results of a survey) and a 90% response rate (which is the percentage of

---

[37]   The number of staff members in August 2005 (I received the data at the beginning of May) was 913, with 615 international staff and 298 local.

[38]   Uma Sekaran, *op. cit.*, page 294

persons in a sample who respond to a survey or the actual percentage of questionnaires completed and returned) were assumed.

So the sample size = (251 x 100%): 90% = 278.88 or 280. The questionnaire was distributed to 186 international staff and to 94 local staff.

Regarding the sample size of the other populations, i.e., the government officers, business people, and the general population, few people were chosen.

3.5 Identification and Specification of all Information Items Needed

The International Criminal Tribunal for Rwanda, as mentioned above, was created to prosecute persons responsible for genocide and other serious violations of international humanitarian law committed in the territory of Rwanda and Rwandan citizens responsible for genocide and other such violations committed in the neighbouring states between 1 January and 31 December 1994.

To enable it to carry out its mission, the General Assembly of the United Nations allocates a biennial budget to the ICTR. A considerable portion of this budget is disbursed on expenditures in the city of Arusha. Thus, for purposes of this research, a considerable amount of information was collected directly from this organization. Other sources of information include:

1. The biennial budgets. These documents are helpful because they provide useful information on the amount of money allocated to the organization, as well as on the organization's proposed expenditures.
2. The financial reports of the ICTR provide us also with information about the expenses of ICTR.

3. Information provided by the procurement section about the vendors of the tribunal based in Arusha.
4. Staff expenditure in the local economy on items like food, accommodation, Tanzanians employed by them, etc.
5. The main suppliers of ICTR on how the presence of the organization has impacted their businesses.
6. The Arusha municipal authority on socio-economic growth of Arusha.

3.6   Data Collection Instruments

For purposes of this study, the data used was based on primary data, which was self-administered to and collected from the staff of ICTR. Some exchanges with the Office of the Director of AICC, the management of the Para-Statal Pensions Fund (real estate in Arusha), some municipality officers, heads of international schools operating in Arusha (Braeburn School and Saint Constantine's International School).

The questionnaire distributed to the staff of ICTR was about their monthly expenditures in the city of Arusha. They were asked, for example, if they employed Tanzanian citizens, the monthly wages they pay to them, the amount they pay monthly for rent, water, electricity, etc.

The questionnaire administered to the management of PPF estates was about the number of ICTR staff tenants they had from 2002 up to 2004, compared to the total number of tenants.

Questions were asked to the director of AICC eliciting general information such as the office space occupied by the ICTR and the corresponding annual rent, etc.

In-depth interviews were also conducted with some officers of The Arusha municipality and some businessmen.

Secondary data from the following sources were also used:

1. The ICTR's expenditures in Arusha, such as the purchase of fuel and payment for insurance premiums for the organization's large fleet of vehicles; purchase of office consumables; rent for the premises; fees paid to international schools in the city of Arusha; etc. Some of the goods and services purchased by the ICTR are made outside Arusha and outside Tanzania, and some of their suppliers are in Dar es Salaam. For purposes of this study, detailed information on purchases made in Tanzania and the addresses of suppliers were requested to help us locate them.

2. The socio-economic profile of Arusha (2004) prepared by the Arusha Municipal Council, gave us some data on the agricultural, industrial, and trade sectors, etc. of the city and its surroundings.

3. The internet, newspapers, and journals gave us information on the literature related to this study.

3.7 Practical Approach for Identifying Individuals to be Interviewed or to Complete the Questionnaire.

The questionnaire administered was structured. The information needed was known. The respondents had enough time to gather the information.

Depending on the type of information we needed, we knew which type of person to interview.

The persons or the managers interviewed, for example, were those we believed would be able to give us some information on the contribution of ICTR to Arusha's economy.

A questionnaire on expenditure patterns was distributed to staff in August 2005. The payroll could have been useful for the selection of people to interview, but because, some staff were on holiday, the questionnaire was distributed from office to office.

Some information regarding the International Criminal Tribunal for Rwanda was collected directly from the relevant heads of department, section of the organization. The data provided by the finance section was sometimes a combination of expenditures made for the Arusha and Kigali offices of the ICTR. According to the chief of the accounts unit of the ICTR, 20% of those expenses were used by the office of ICTR in Kigali. We therefore deducted those 20% to arrive at the portion allocated to the Arusha headquarters. Most of the information used was provided by the procurement unit.

3.8   Data Analysis Methods Used

To determine ICTR's contribution to Arusha's economy, this study uses a model that examines how spending enters the Arusha municipality as a result of ICTR's existence here.

A major premise of ICTR contribution models is that the ICTR is considered to be part of the export sector of the local economy. The rationale behind this is that the revenue of the ICTR comes from outside of the local economy. In the absence of the ICTR, these non-local funds would have been spent elsewhere. Thus, to the extent that these non-local sources of funds are spent locally, the ICTR is responsible for income being spent in the local economy.

The methodology is based on a cash-flow model that focuses on expenditures, namely the spending of the ICTR, its employees, lawyers, and interns. The aggregate spending from these sources provides a reasonable approximation of the total cash flow injected into the local business as a result of ICTR's presence in Arusha.

The questionnaire received from ICTR staff, was cleaned, coded, and analysed using MS Excel software. Descriptive statistics were done to get the mean and the standard deviation of every type of expense. The mean gives an idea of the average spent per month by every staff member. The mean of every type of expense was then multiplied by the total number of staff to have an idea of total spending on that particular item. Graphs and histograms were also used.

Concerning the data on expenses of the ICTR, goods and services were divided into three different categories: expenses in Arusha, expenses in Tanzania, and expenses outside Tanzania. This gave an idea of the proportion of expenses made in Arusha compared to the total expense.

3.9   Constraints and Limitations

The main limitation of this study was the access to sufficient economic data that could have made possible a comprehensive analysis of the impact.

Some sources of ICTR expenditures are not always detailed. This means that there is not always precision on how much was spent in Arusha and how much was spent in other offices of ICTR. It was not possible, for example, to have information on the amount spent by the tribunal in travel tickets. According to the chief of the ICTR accounts unit, 80% of every category of expenses reported in ICTR's books represents expenses for Arusha. Unfortunately, this really doesn't reflect the expenses made in Arusha.

The survey distributed to employees doesn't represent the real expenses of the staff. It was difficult to capture those expenses, and staff were just estimating the amount spent. For this reason, the net portion of the salary paid to staff by the tribunal, as well as the net salary paid to national staff, were included in the contribution made by ICTR. The survey was integrated just to make an estimate of the amount spent by the staff. However, the answers to the survey on the number of Tanzanians they employ in their houses as well as the salaries paid to them were more accurate.

Secondly, businesses contacted were not willing to release their information, citing confidentiality as a reason or fearing disclosure to the competition.

Obtaining information on the economic profile of the city of Arusha over a given period of time has also been impossible. There seems to be no such monograph. Existing literature on Arusha was not available. This difficulty in itself constitutes an obstacle to the conduct of a comprehensive study on the impact of the presence and operations of the ICTR on the city's economy because of the lack of references, benchmarks on the trend of the economic growth, price index, etc.

Further, the multiplier effect of ICTR expenditures was not computed due to the lack of authoritative value of the multiplier.

Due to the scope and limitations of this study, other categories of additional economic contributions remain for further study. These additional contributions would include visitor spending (these are ICTR's visitors and visits of staff's family and friends) and expert's and consultant's expenses, etc.

CHAPTER 4

DATA ANALYSIS AND EVALUATION

4.1   Introduction

This chapter is concerned mainly with the contribution the ICTR made to the local economy. The chapter first presents the revenue sources of the ICTR. This is followed by the direct contribution of ICTR through its huge procurement operations, salaries and wages, rental of its premises, running of a detention facility, etc. Finally, we consider the expenditures generated by the ICTR to pay its staff. The ICTR also purchased goods and services outside the area of Arusha, and the economic effects were felt in the region from which the supplies were imported. Those expenditures that "leak" out of Arusha would not be included in estimating the economic contribution of ICTR at the local level. However, before looking at how the ICTR contributed to the local economy, we will first of all identify the sources of its revenues.

4.2   Sources of Revenues

Like other United Nations institutions, the ICTR relies upon member states of the world organization to contribute the funds needed to finance its activities. The ICTR is financed in two ways, through assessed and voluntary contributions. The former are paid for by member states, whereas the latter are contributed by states, intergovernmental and non-governmental organizations, and even individuals.[39] Assessed contributions are supported through mandatory contributions of member states. Half of the ICTR's regular budget is assessed according

---

[39]   See Resolution 955 (1994) of the UN Security Council establishing the ICTR.

to the general UN scale of assessment applicable to the regular budget; the other half is assessed according to the scale of assessment applicable to UN peace-keeping operations.[40]

The ICTR assessed or regular budgets are adopted on a biennial basis[41] as per the following procedure.

The process begins within the ICTR itself developing proposed activities and spending for the coming budgetary cycle. Contributions from the various organs (chambers, office of the prosecutor, and registry) are put together in the UN approved format by the chief of the Division of Administrative Support Services of the registry.

The draft document is submitted to the Department of Management at the UN headquarters in New York, more specifically to its Office of Program Planning, Budget, and Accounts (OPPBA). Then follow protracted exchanges between the latter and the ICTR, aimed at ensuring compliance with the fiscal guidelines set by the Secretary General and the General Assembly. Once this is done, the document is submitted to the General Assembly as a report of the Secretary General, containing resource requirements of the ICTR for the budgetary cycle concerned. From the moment the request goes to the General Assembly, it becomes subject to intense intergovernmental politics.[42] The first choke-point is the Advisory Committee on Administrative and Budgetary Questions (ACABQ), a standing panel of eighteen individuals elected for a three-year term by the General Assembly for their expertise in fiscal policy and public administration. The major functions of the Advisory Committee are:

[40] UN Office of Programme Planning, Budget and Accounts (Department of Management), Budgeting in the United Nations, http://www.un.org/ga/60/fifth/pbudget.htm

[41] This is the case since the year xxx. Before that date the budget appropriations were annual.

[42] Jeffrey Laurenti, "Financing the United Nations, International Relations Studies and the UN," *Occasional Papers*, 2001 number 2

1. To examine and report on the budget submitted by the Secretary General to the General Assembly,
2. To advise the General Assembly on any administrative and budgetary matters referred to it.
3. To examine on behalf of the General Assembly the administrative budgets of the specialized agencies and proposals for financial arrangements with such agencies.
4. To consider and report to the General Assembly on the auditors' reports on the accounts of the United Nations and of the specialized agencies.[43]

Although technically presented as an "advisory" panel, the ACABQ is the primary budgetary decision-making organ in the UN political process. Its "recommendations" are generally accepted as baselines by the Fifth Committee of the UN General Assembly[44], which is the next body to review the resources requirements of the ICTR.

The Fifth Committee is the main committee of the General Assembly entrusted with responsibilities for administration and budgetary matters. It is composed of representatives of all member states. Their role is to work out the required political deals to reach an agreement on budgetary matters under review. Once a budget is approved in the Fifth Committee, its final adoption by the General Assembly—which is composed of the same member states—is generally a formality.

---

[43] www.un.org/docs/acabq
[44] This committee is in charge of administrative and financial issues. The other standing committees of the General Assembly are as follows: First Committee (disarmament and international security), Second Committee (economic and financial affairs), Third Committee (social, humanitarian and cultural affairs), Fourth Committee (special political affairs and decolonization), and Sixth Committee (legal affairs).

4.3   Assessment of the Direct Contribution of the ICTR

The ICTR expenditures can be broadly divided into the following categories: the expenditure originated by the ICTR itself for its maintenance and operations, those involving salaries paid to its staff, stipends paid to legal researchers, and daily subsistence allowance (DSA) paid to the defence teams.

4.3.1   Expenditure on Maintenance and Operations

Before 2002, a huge amount of money was spent by ICTR to set up the tribunal. The courtrooms and the premises used for the detention of detainees, for example, were built, with most of the materials used being bought on the local market and the building contractors hired from the local market. The premises hosting the headquarters were renovated, etc. Further, since 2002 the ICTR is still spending a huge amount of money for its maintenance and operations. Part of this amount was spent locally and part externally. The breakdown of these expenditures will help us to know the proportion of money used to purchase goods and services in Arusha.

4.3.1.1 Local Expenditure on Maintenance and Operations

In the course of its activities, the International Criminal Tribunal for Rwanda received from the General Assembly, a total amount of $204,365,100 for the biennium 2002-2003 and the revised amount of $255,909,500 for the biennium 2004-2005.[45] Extra budgetary resources amounting to $2,368,600 for the biennium 2002-2003 and $2,723,900 for the biennium 2004-2005 were also provided by member states. The final budget used for the biennium 2002-03 amounted to $206,733,700, and the revised budget for the biennium 2004-05 amounted to $258,633,400.

---

[45]   Information provided by the ICTR Budget Officer. The budget is in thousands of United States dollars

Part of the amount received was spent on paying salaries, honoraria, and fees to employees, judges, defence counsel, consultants, and experts. Another part was used for the rent and maintenance of premises—ICTR is located in the Arusha International Conference Centre (AICC) building[46]—and for rent of other premises occupied by the organization to host witnesses who come from all over the world to testify before the tribunal. Other expenses covered the purchase of goods and services from the local market or from outside. The procurement of goods and services in the local market includes payment for utilities, communications, security services, contractual services, supplies, and materials.

The ICTR has built within the compound of the Tanzanian correctional centre in Kisongo-Arusha, a United Nations Detention Facility (UNDF), which conforms to international standards. This detention facility holds 57 detainees.[47] During the year 2002, for example, the ration for these detainees was estimated at $105,480,190 $111,526,220 for the year 2003 and $85,599,434 from January 2004 up August 2004.[48]

---

[46] www.aicc.co.tz "The AICC was established under the Public Corporation's Act, 1969, by a Presidential Order, i.e. The Arusha International Conference Centre (Establishment Order), issued vide Government Notice Number 115, published on 25th August 1978. AICC is under a 100% government ownership but operates as a fully-fledged commercial entity without any subsidies from the Central Government." Its main objective is to manage and control the Headquarters Complex of the defunct East Africa Community (EAC) and other premises and lands in Arusha municipality and to provide facilities and services in the complex for the purpose of conferences, meetings, etc.

[47] As of 30 September 2005; www.ictr.org/default.htm

[48] Information provided by the commander of the United Nations Detention Facility, ICTR

The ICTR has also set up a medical clinic within its headquarters. A lot of drugs are purchased in the local market to cater for the medical needs of the staff, their dependents, and the detainees.

Other expenses made by the tribunal are the rations and clothes for the witnesses and the dry cleaning and laundry for all ICTR-Arusha linen, such as bed sheets, pillows, blankets, doctor's coats, towels, curtains, uniforms, etc.

According to information received from the ICTR, the local spending on goods and services in Arusha were as follows.

Over the period of January to December 2002, $3,585,112 was spent. It peaked to $8,386,881 over the period of January 2003 to December 2004 and was down to $4,189,641.79 from January 2004 to December 2004. Below is the table of estimated local procurement.

ICTR's purchases of goods and services from 2002 to 2004 were estimated at $16,161,634.40

Table 4.1: Overall Level of ICTR Spending in Arusha
(2002, 2003, and 2004)

Years	2002	2003	2004	Total
Rental of premises	$1,322,644	$1,437,187	$1,450,110	$4,209,940
Communication & Utilities (electricity, water, fuel)	$628,882	$935,337	$873,270	$2,437,489
Materials, Supplies, other procurements & contractual services	$840,918	$5,008,808	$1,038,991	$6,888,717
Office furniture	$29,114	$174,184	$92,770	$296,068
Security Services	$575,334	$674,029	$603,987	$1,853,350

Bank Charges	$176,093	$135,169	$140,837	$416099
Insurance	$12,127.4210	$22,167.09	$25,677.08	$59,971.59
Sub-total	$3,585,112	$8,386,881	$4,189,642	$16,161,634

Source: ICTR

ICTR also purchased goods and services in other areas of Tanzania such as Dar es Salaam and Moshi. The said expenses cover mainly computers and internet services and aircraft operations. The ICTR rents on a permanent basis an aircraft mainly to cater for the travel needs of its witnesses and staff between Arusha and Kigali, Rwanda. The rented aircraft is also used for the transfer to Arusha of some of the accused persons arrested on the African continent. The operation of the aircraft involves the payment of parking and landing fees, clearing, and forwarding taxes for the ICTR. Table 4.2 below shows the expenses incurred by the ICTR in Tanzania but out of Arusha and its surroundings.

Table 4.2: Estimated Level of ICTR Spending in
Other Areas of Tanzania

Years	2002	2003	2004	Total
Aircraft operations (landing, parking and ground handling)	$18,000	$18,000	$18,000	$54,000
Other expenses	$44,093	$ 66,0136	$702,075	$1,406,303
Sub-Total	$62,093	$678,136	$720,075	$1,460,303

Source: ICTR

ICTR's purchases of goods and services in Dar es Salaam and Moshi in Tanzania amounted to $62,093 for the year 2002, $678,136 for the year 2003, and $720,075 for the year 2004. The total expenditures from January 2002 to December 2004 were estimated at $1,460,303. This study indicates that 92% of the expenditures in Tanzania were made in Arusha and surrounding areas and 8% out of Arusha and its environs.

4.3.1.2 External Spending on Maintenance and Operations.

Although ICTR is located in Arusha, a considerable part of its expenses occur out of Tanzania. Its purchases are made based on the quality and prices of the product offered by foreign suppliers. The organization purchased goods and services from the United Kingdom, France, United Arab Emirates, United States of America, Kenya, etc.

The major external expenditure of ICTR was made on communications equipment, audio-visual equipment, acquisition of vehicles and spare parts, library books, etc. Based on the information received from ICTR, the expenses made out of Tanzania are presented in the table below.

Table 4.3: ICTR Spending outside Tanzania

Years	External Spending (USD)
2002	3,777,633
2003	40,994,862
2004	6,555,245
Total	51,327,740

Source: ICTR

Of the overall spending of ICTR on goods and services, 23% was spent in the local market—this means in Arusha and its surrounding areas—2% in Dar es Salaam and Moshi and 74% out of Tanzania.

Figure 4.1: Breakdown of Expenditure Shares 2002-2004 in Arusha, in Tanzanian and outside Tanzania

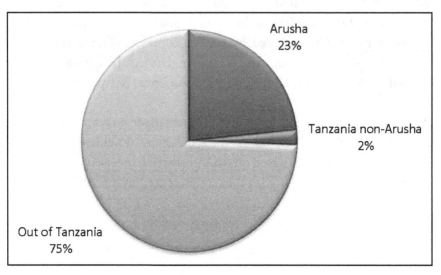

Source: Author's Estimates from ICTR Data

4.3.2   ICTR Expenditures on Staff

A major source of economic activity associated with the ICTR's presence in Arusha is the spending by national and international staff. In this study we assumed that wages paid to national staff are used in the local market. It was very difficult to work out the exact amount spent in the local market by staff. We assumed that this local portion[49] of the international employees' salary was used in the local market.

---

[49]   Internationally recruited staff members are allowed to opt for the payment of a portion of their monthly salary into an account hosted by a foreign bank of their choice.

4.3.2.1 National Employee Wages and Medical Insurance Plan

Employment of national staff is one of the most direct contributions made by ICTR. Expenditure on national staff salaries accounted for $6,695,614 from January 2002 to December 2004.

In 2002, 208 posts were occupied by Tanzanian citizens, and the net salary paid to them was $2,178,919. The net salary here is the total earnings[50] of the staff minus the staff assessment.

In 2003, 227 Tanzanian were recruited and received a net salary of $2,043,760. In 2004, 232 posts were occupied by Tanzanians, who received a total net salary of $2,472,935.

Table 4.4: Total Expenditure of ICTR on National Staff
(Net Salary)

Year	Number of Local Staff Employed	Net Salary
2002	208	$2,178,918.79
2003	227	$2,043,759.66
2004	232	$2,472,935.21
Total		$ 6,695,613.66

Source: ICTR

The total net salary paid to the national staff between 2002 and 2004, as shown by this table amounts to $6,695,614

The United Nations introduced with effect from 1 September 1987, the Medical Insurance Plan (MIP)[51]. It provides automatic health

---

[50] The total earnings include the gross salary, the medical Insurance plan subsidy, the pension fund, and the dependency allowance.

[51] United Nations, Secretariat, Document Secretariat/AI/343, 31 July 1987. Administrative Instruction from the Controller to members of the staff at designated duty stations away from Headquarters. Subject: Medical

insurance for United Nations' locally recruited staff members and, on an optional basis, for their eligible family members. This MIP is applicable to Tanzanian staff working with the tribunal. For one insured person, for example, the subscriber's contribution represents one quarter and that of the organization's three quarters of the total premium.

Table 4.5: MIP Paid by ICTR to Locally Recruited Staff

Years	ICTR's Contribution
2002	$133,477
2003	$134,809
2004	$154,314
Total	$422,599

Source: ICTR

During the period covered by the study, an estimated amount of $7,118,213 was spent by the tribunal on wages and MIP-related costs for its locally recruited staff.

4.3.2.2 Wages of international Staff and Education Grant

Another way in which resources are injected into the local market is through spending by international staff. International staff have the option of receiving a portion of their salary in Arusha and the other portion in a foreign bank of their choice. A survey was undertaken in the framework of this research to determine the level of expenses made by the international staff in Arusha. Most of the staff members do not keep accurate records of their spending in Arusha on household items, for example.[52] The following is the local portion paid to international staff. The judges are not included in the number of ICTR staff presented below. They receive the total amount of their salary here in Arusha and it was assumed to be fully used in Arusha.

Insurance Plan for Locally Recruited Staff at Designated Duty Stations away from Headquarters.

[52] The survey will be discussed at a later stage.

Table 4.6: Net Local Portion Paid by ICTR
to International Staff

Year	Number of Staff	Total Portion Intern. Staff
2002	362	$8,459,847
2003	413	$10,453,657
2004	452	$14,179,999
Total		$33,093,503

Source: ICTR

From January 2002 to December 2004, a total amount of $33,093,503 was disbursed to staff members in Arusha as the local portion of their salaries. The figure could have been further refined if data was available, for example, on the money transfers made by international staff from their foreign accounts to cater for expenses in Arusha, or on expenses made outside of Arusha financed from the local portion of their salaries.

Another type of expenses made by the ICTR on its international staff is in the form of the payment of education grants, travel tickets for their home leave, or alternate leave entitlements. Since the ICTR was not in a position to provide us with the required information on the amount spent on travel tickets, this item was excluded from this study. With regard to the education grants, the ICTR reimburses up to 75% of the education costs of international staff members' eligible dependents.

The amount of $2,561,014 was spent on education grant payments in Arusha from January 2002 to December 2004 through the refund made to parents by the tribunal and the amount paid by the parents. At the time this study was being finalized, some education grant reimbursements were still being processed by the tribunal. This means that the total amount spent on education grant is higher than the figure provided above. According to the ICTR records as confirmed by the survey undertaken under this study, the following institutions are the main beneficiaries of educational expenses made by the ICTR and its internationally recruited employees: Braeburn School Tanzania Limited, International School of Moshi (Arusha Campus), St Constantine's International School.

Table 4.7: Education Grant for Students Attending
School in Arusha

School Year	Amount Refunded by ICTR to Parents	Differential Paid by Parents to Schools	Total Amount Paid
2002	$558,809	$186,270	$745,078
2003	$690,974	$230,325	$921,298
2004	$670,978	$223,659	$894,637
Total	$1,920,760	$640,253	$2,561,014

Source: ICTR and Author's Survey

Based on the above, a total of $35,654,517 was injected in the local economy through the salary and education grants paid to ICTR international staff.

In sum, from January 2002 to December 2004, the total amount of $42,772,730 was injected into the local economy under the following headings: wages of locally recruited staff, local portion of internationally recruited staff, medical insurance plan premiums, and educational fees paid to schools.

4.3.2.3 Expenditures on Legal Researchers.

The ICTR runs an internship program through which it brings to Arusha interns who are able to pay for their travel, living, and other expenses. The only assistance they receive from the ICTR is their free transportation from the Kilimanjaro Airport to Arusha on arrival and back on departure, as well as their daily transport to and from the office.

The ICTR also runs a legal researchers' program, under which selected young lawyers receive financial assistance from the tribunal in the form of a roundtrip air ticket to and from Arusha (up to a maximum of US $1,500 per ticket) and a monthly stipend of $1,100 for six months. This program is only open to citizens from the developing world (Africa, Asia, South America, the Pacific Region, Indian Ocean Region, etc.) who have completed a law degree.

Interns and legal researchers are responsible for their own accommodation and living expenses during their assignment to the tribunal. According to the information received from ICTR, the tribunal has hosted 313 interns and 67 legal researchers between 2002 and 2004.

For purposes of this research, we have taken into account only the expenses made by the legal researchers since they are the only ones receiving stipends from the tribunal. It is also assumed that the stipend received is used in Arusha for their accommodation. The amount spent on their air ticket is not covered by the study, since the ICTR was not in a position to provide us with precise figures on this item. Based on this assumption, the ICTR spent the amount of $73,700 to cater for the living expenses of its legal researchers in Arusha from January 2002 to December 2004.

4.3.2.4. Defence Counsel

Under the ICTR statute and relevant regulations, a defence team should be paid by the organization to assist indigent accused persons. All the accused persons held to date by the tribunal have been considered to be indigent.

To qualify to be assigned to represent the interest of an accused person, candidates should be admitted to the practice of law in a state or be a university professor of law. Detailed eligibility criteria, as well as other important regulations concerning the ICTR legal aid program, are contained in the ICTR's Directive on the Assignment of Defence Counsel.

As per article 17 of this directive, where counsel has been assigned, the cost and expenses of legal representation of the suspect or accused necessarily and reasonably incurred shall be met by the tribunal. Such costs and expenses shall include costs relating to investigative and procedural steps, measures taken for the production of evidence to assist or support the defence, expenses for ascertainment of facts, consultancy and expert opinion, transportation and accommodation of witnesses, postal charges, registration fees, taxes or similar duties, and all remuneration due to counsel. The remuneration paid includes: a fixed rate, fees calculated on the basis of a fixed hourly rate based on the counsel's seniority and experience, and a daily subsistence allowance based on the United Nations Schedule of Daily Subsistence Allowance Rates in force at the time when work is done.

The study has considered only the DSA paid to assigned counsel, since it is supposed to cater for defence teams' stays while in Arusha. We have considered $100 per day as our assumption.

The defence teams in ICTR are generally composed of five persons: the lead counsel, the co-counsel, assistant (s), and investigator (s). Every team has the option to choose between two assistants and one investigator or two investigators and one assistant. Each of them is also entitled to a DSA during their stay in Arusha.

Between January 2002 and December 2004, eight cases were completed, on appeal, or in progress involving 38 accused persons. Some of the cases involved more than one accused, such as the *Butare Case* with six accused persons and the *Military I Case* with four. Because some defence teams are composed of fewer than five members, we chose to use $350 as DSA per team per day, and not $ 500. To have the estimated DSA paid to them, the number of days spent by teams in Arusha was multiplied by 350. The estimated DSA spent by the ICTR on DSA to the defence teams from January 2002 to December 2004 was $428,750.

Because of the presence of ICTR in Arusha, $428,750 was injected into the local economy through the DSA paid to the defence teams.

The total amount injected through the procurement of goods and services by the direct purchases of ICTR, the purchases of its staff, interns, legal researchers, and defence teams is estimated to be $58,796,561.

Figure 4.2: Breakdown of ICTR and its Community's Contribution to the Local Economy.

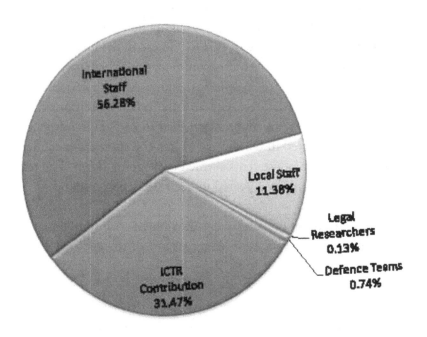

Source: Author's Estimates

The results of the survey undertaken as part of this research on spending of local and international staff indicate that the purchasing power of the ICTR employees also had a considerable impact on employment creation in Arusha.

4.4   Assessment of how the Salary Earned by Staff is Used

The International Criminal Tribunal for Rwanda spent a total amount of $39,789,117 to pay its national and international staff. This money, as it will be seen, was used on household, expenditures, employment of domestic staff, etc.

4.4.1   International Staff Expenditures.

4.4.1.1 Spending on House Rent

Since the establishment of the ICTR, a considerable number of residential houses have been built in the city. The *Arusha Times* anticipated in 1995 the inflow of roughly 400 staff, visitors, and residents due to the presence of ICTR. "These individuals will require either residential houses or hotel accommodation which means a lot of money will be coming into Arusha"[53], it added. After the establishment of ICTR, rents started to escalate and the rental conditions became more drastic. Three to six months' rent had to be paid in advance and was generally expected in US dollars. When the survey was conducted in August 2005, the house rents seemed to be going down. The reason seemed to be that supply appeared to be greater than demand.

Three hundred questionnaires were distributed to international staff. 186 surveys were received, representing 100% of the targeted response rate.

Based on the data collected from the survey, rent levels of the houses rented by international staff vary between $250 and $1500. Three per cent of the staff owned their own houses. Forty three per cent of the staff paid between $500 and $750 for accommodation, while those paying more than $1,250 were 3% of the sample.

---

53   The *Arusha Times*, September 1-15, 1995, No 1.

The sample mean, which is $702, was multiplied by the entire population of the international staff. This gave us a total amount of $336,774 spent monthly by staff on rent. A few years back, rent levels were higher than the price shown by this survey. The total amount could therefore have been higher than $336,774.

Table 4.8: House Rent

Monthly rent	Number of Respondents	Percentage
Under $250	8	4
$250 but under $500	26	14
$500 but under $750	80	43
$750 but under $1,000	51	27
$1,000 but under $1,250	15	8
$1,250 but under $1,500	6	3

Source: Staff Survey

The tribunal is expected to be closed in 2010, and staff downsizing will start in 2008. While conducting the survey, it was noticed that, for security reasons and others, international staff are moving from bungalows to apartments. This type of accommodation probably explains why 43% of the staff rent is between $500 and $750. Below is the result of a survey carried out with the management of two of the biggest estates that house a considerable number of international staff and are owned by the Para-Statal Pensions Fund.

The Parastatal Pensions Fund (PPF)[54] had invested in real estate in Arusha. The PPF management noticed that there was a great demand

---

[54] www.ppftz.org. "Para-Statal Pensions Fund is a pension fund, which was established by Act, 14 of 1978 for the purpose of providing pensions and other related benefits to its members". "Contributions collected are invested based on the fund's investment policy, which specifies three broad investments areas, namely fixed income asset, equities and properties".

for houses by foreigners coming to work with ICTR and built furnished houses to facilitate their installation. There are two residential estates, namely PPF Oloirien Estate and PPF Kaloleni Estate. Those estates have the capacity to accommodate more than 100 families and are equipped with stand-by generators and 24-hours water supply, and they are well secured. According to information provided by the management of these estates, the rent for PPF Oloirien varies between $800 and $1,600, service charge included. In 2002, 52% of the residents were ICTR staff, in 2003 they were 57% and in 2004, they were 62%.

Ninety per cent of the tenants in Kololeni Estate were ICTR staff in 2002, 2003, and 2004 and the rent, inclusive of service charges per month, was $560.

Table 4.9: Percentage of ICTR's Staff Living in PPF estates

Year	No of Houses/Flats	ICTR Staff	Percentage
2002	110	65	59
2004	110	69	62
2004	110	74	67

Source: PPF

Put together, the occupancy rate by ICTR staff for the two estates was as follows: in 2002 it was 59%; 62% in 2003; and 67% in 2004.

This study gives an idea of how the presence of ICTR benefited the real estate sector in Arusha. Thanks to this good health, PPF employs 123 people in its estates, including 44 Security guards, 67 gardeners, and 12 management staff.

4.4.1.2 Creation of Employment and Spending on Domestic Staff

The presence of ICTR in Arusha has created a considerable number of jobs not only for local staff employed by the tribunal (ICTR employed 208 local staff in 2002, 227 in 2003, and 232 in 2004), but also for other Tanzanian citizens. These employments could have been created by businesses supplying goods and services to ICTR, by the real estate sector, etc. The international staff also created a huge number of employment opportunities for house helps, gardeners, security guards, etc.

According to the results of our survey, 1,597 employments were created by the entire international staff, including 619 (39%) house helps, 301 (19%) gardeners, 632 (40%) security guards, and 49(3%) drivers. It should, however, be observed that there would be more security guards if service charges were not included in the rent of some houses.

The salary paid to the house helps varied from less than $50 to more than $250.[55] The total monthly amount paid to house helps was $41,161, representing 32% of the salary paid monthly to domestic servants.

Gardeners were paid between less than $50 and more than $150.[56] The total monthly amount paid to gardeners was estimated to be $24,000. (19% of the total amount paid monthly to domestic staff).

Drivers, with a salary varying also between less than $50 and more than $150, received from the international staff a total monthly salary of $4,065 (3% of the total monthly salary paid to domestic staff).

Finally, with regard to security guards, it was really difficult to get the exact amount paid directly to them. Some international staff hire security guards from security companies and pay directly to the companies. The salary we registered was between less than $50 and more than $400. The estimated monthly amount paid was $57,548 (45% of the total amount

---

[55] Most of the house helpers who were paid less than $50 were working half-time. When a staff had more than one house helper, the sum of the amount paid to them was made. This is why there are amounts between $100 and more than $200 paid to them.

[56] When they was more than one gardener, their salary was summed and generally gave more than $100.

paid monthly to domestic staff). We assumed that this amount was included in the expenses made by staff. Regarding security, since 2005, the tribunal has been paying $300 to international staff to cover the cost of the panic buttons or security alarm systems and security guards.

In conclusion, the international staff created 1,597 employments in Arusha and injected a total monthly amount of $126,774 through salary paid to their staff.

4.4.1.3 Other Expenses Generated by International Staff

Household items (food, beverage, etc.) and fuel consumption are the areas where a lot of money was spent by staff. Depending on the number of person(s) in each family, the household expenditure varied from under $200 to over $1,400, amounting to a total of $265,807 spent monthly by the entire staff on household items.

The average number of cars per staff was 1.2, with 4% of the respondents being without cars, 74% with one car, 19% with two cars, and 2% with three cars. This gave a total number of 573 cars owned by international staff. The fuel consumed is estimated to be $61,548 per month.

The monthly amount spent on cable television subscriptions was estimated at $28,903; $52,129 on telephone bills; $11,716 on water bills, $31,381 on electricity bills; and $17,858 on internet connections.

Table 4.10 Average Monthly International Staff
Spending on the Local Market

Category	UDS per month	Percentage
Domestic Staff	126,774	13
Rent	336,774	36
Household	265,807	28
Fuel	61,548	7

Television	28,903	3
Telephone	52,129	6
Water	11,716	1
Electricity	31,381	3
Internet	17,858	2
Total	932,890	100

Source: Staff Survey

Figure 4.3: Average Monthly Expenses of
International Staff in Arusha

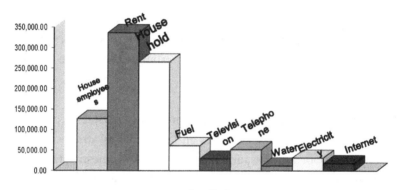

$ per Month

Source: Staff Survey

Regarding the amounts spent on childcare activities (after-school programs), medical care (hospital and pharmacy), auto repairs costs, and entertainment, there were just a few answers. This item was therefore not integrated in the expenses made by the staff. However, it was noticed during our survey that a lot of children had tuition after school and took other lessons such as music, swimming, tennis, etc.

International staff are also members of clubs where they pay membership fees.

International staff spend also some money on the school fees of their children. They pay the school fees to the schools, and 75% of these fees

329

are reimbursed by the tribunal. In the last school year (2004-2005), for example, parents paid $640,253 in addition to the $1,920,760 paid by the tribunal.

Some staff members are involved in *pro bono* activities and also spent some of their money in charitable activities.

4.4.1.4 Staff Voluntary and Charitable Activities

ICTR employees also undertake voluntary activities within Arusha. Over 33% of the surveyed respondents indicated spending some time on voluntary activities. Examples provided included religious activities, sport coaching, parents' associations, etc. In all, a total of 157 employees representing 33% of the international staff are engaged in these voluntary activities.

Of the staff, 64% indicated that they provided charitable contributions to local organizations like churches and orphanages, street children and assistance to poor families, and tuition fees for domestic staff, etc. The gap between the amounts spent yearly by the various staff members on this item was so wide that it was very difficult to compute it. For example, while some staff spent less than $50 per year, others spent more than $5,000. Between $600 and less than $1,000, data was not available.

The information from the monthly expenses was combined to estimate the total direct contribution made by international staff members. Employees directly spent an estimated amount of $932,890 in the Arusha area.

This amount should be higher than this if all expenditure items were surveyed.

4.4.2 National Staff Expenditures

This part covers the same expenditures made by international staff.

4.4.2.1 Spending on Domestic Staff

The Tanzanian staff of the ICTR contributed a large amount to the economy of their country. According to the results of our survey, they spent a total amount of Tshs 20,147,340 on personnel working in their residences. Out of this amount, Tshs 7,454,255 went to house helps, Tshs 4,065,957 went to gardeners, Tshs 5,343,085 went to security guards, and Tshs 3,284,042 went to drivers. A total of 375 employments were created by these local staff.

4.4.2.2 Other Expenses Made by Tanzanian Staff

The other estimated expenses made by Tanzanian staff were on the rent of their houses (Tshs 20,069,139); household items (Tshs 47,045,213); fuel (Tshs 17,853,723); television subscriptions (Tshs 4,535,106); telephone (Tshs 12,458,511); water (Tshs 3,857,447); electricity (Tshs 7,662,766); and internet connections (Tshs 286,702).

Table 4.11: Average monthly Tanzanian Staff' Expenditures

Category	Tshs per Month	USD per Month (Tshs 1135 = $1)[57]	Percentage
Domestic Staff	20,147,340	17,751	15
Rent	20,069,149	17,682	15
Household	47,045,213	41,450	35
Fuel	17,853,723	15,730	13
Television	4,535,106	3,996	3
Telephone	12,458,511	10,977	9
Water	3,857,447	3,399	3
Electricity	7662,766	6,751	6
Internet	286,702	253	0.2
Total	133,915,957	117,988	100%

Source: Staff Survey

---

[57] 2005 United Nations Operational Rate of Exchange, provided by the ICTR

Figure 4.4.: Average Monthly Expenses of Local Staff

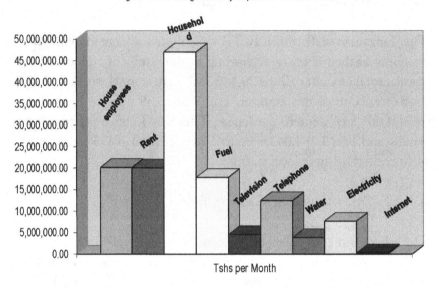

Tshs per Month

The estimated monthly amount spent by Tanzanian staff in the local market was estimated to be Tshs 133,915,957 or $117,988.

According to the results of our survey, 90% of these staff were employed before joining the tribunal. Their monthly net salary varied between less than Tshs 50,000 ($44) to more than Tshs 450,000 ($396). The total monthly salaries paid to the entire Tanzanian staff at that time by their various employers was estimated at Tshs 40,398,936 or $35,594 (at the average exchange rate of August, i.e. Tshs 1,135 for $1)

After joining the tribunal, their net salaries varied between Tshs 500,000 ($441) and more than Tshs 2,500,000 ($2203). The total monthly salary paid to the entire Tanzanian workforce by the ICTR was estimated at Tshs 293,218,085 or $258,342.

4.4.2.3 Voluntary and Charitable Activities

Twenty per cent of survey respondents undertake voluntary activities within Arusha. This figure represents 50% of the number of local staff giving some of their time for voluntary activities.

Eighty six per cent of the survey respondents indicated that they undertook activities and made contributions to local organizations like churches and orphanages and otherwise provided assistance to people in need.

CHAPTER 5

SUMMARY, CONCLUSIONS, AND RECOMMENDATIONS

5.1   Introduction

A considerable number of items were covered by this study on the contribution made by the International Criminal Tribunal of Rwanda to the local economy. This chapter will focus first on the summary of the study. It will then draw conclusions from previous chapters and finally make some recommendations to the tribunal in particular and to the United Nations' operations in general, as well as to the Tanzanian government, its various arms, and other stakeholders.

5.2   Summary

This study was undertaken to provide an estimation of the economic benefits of the tribunal's presence as a functioning organization within Arusha. The tribunal's presence was evaluated in terms of the direct and indirect monetary benefits to the Arusha community and the impact of these benefits on employment within Arusha. The research also attempted to estimate the expenditure made by the staff of the tribunal.

The key findings are summarised below.

5.2.1   Key Findings

5.2.1.1 The Contribution of ICTR

The study found that the ICTR spent $16,161,634 on its maintenance and operations in Arusha and surrounding areas. This amount represented only 23% of the total amount spent. In other cities of Tanzania 2% was spent while 74% was spent in towns outside Tanzania.

The other contribution made by ICTR is the education grant paid to the dependent children of the international staff. This was estimated to be $1,920,760. (Some education grants were still being processed when the information was given.)

The tribunal contributes also an estimated amount of $422,599 to the health insurance of locally recruited general service staff.

The total contribution of ICTR was estimated to be $18,504,994. This amount could have been more if information on travel were available.

5.2.1.2 The Contribution of International Staff

The contribution of international staff was through the net local portion of their salaries received here in Arusha. It was found that from January 2002 to December 2004, $33,093,50 was paid to them. It was assumed that this amount was spent in Arusha and surrounding areas. The survey of these employees revealed that they spent $932,890 per month in Arusha.

5.2.1.3 The Contribution of Local Staff

During the same period, $6,695,61 was paid to the national staff. It was also assumed that this amount was spent in Arusha and its environs. This salary represented 17% of the total salary paid to the international and local staff here in Arusha. The survey made on this staff revealed that they spent Tshs133,915,957 or $117,988 a month on their rent, utilities, etc. in Arusha

5.2.1.4 The Contribution of Legal Researchers and Defence Counsel

Legal researchers are young lawyers financially sponsored by the tribunal and brought to Arusha for a six-month period. From January 2002 to December 2004, $73,700 was disbursed for their accommodation.

During the same period $428,750 was paid to Defence teams for their daily subsistence allowance (DSA). These two categories received a total amount of $502,450.

5.2.1.5 Other Contributions

The education sector is one of the sectors benefiting from the presence of ICTR. In addition to what was reimbursed by the tribunal, parents contributed $640,253 for the education of their children. This represents 25% of the total amount introduced into the local education sector, estimated at $2,561,013.

The study also found that 64% of international staff and 86% of local staff made contributions to local charitable organizations. Fifty per cent of local staff and 33% of international staff also undertook voluntary activities in Arusha.

5.2.1.6 Creation of Employment

Apart from the ICTR, which directly created 208 employments in 2002, 227 in 2003, and 232 in 2004, the purchasing power of staff had a considerable employment-generating effect.

According to the results of the survey undertaken in the framework of this research in August 2005, the international staff had created

1597 employees, out of which 39% were hired as house helps, 19% as gardeners, 40% as security guards, and 3% as drivers.

According to the same survey, the locally recruited staff created 375 employment positions, out of which 37% were employed as house helps, 20% as gardeners, 27% as security guards, and 16% as drivers.

5.2.1.7 The Total Direct Spending of ICTR

The study reveals that the estimated total direct impact of ICTR, including its expenses on goods and services and those spent by its community (staff, legal researchers, and defence counsels) from January 2002 to December 2004 was $58,796,561.

5.3   Conclusion

With the establishment of the ICTR, a huge amount of money had been introduced into the local economy as a consequence of its operations.

Government officials acknowledge that the presence of the ICTR has boosted the economy of Arusha. Local businesses continue to find ICTR and its community key to the success of their business.

In one of its issues, the *Arusha Times*[58] interviewed a few people about the pains and joys of the ICTR exit. According to one of the persons interviewed, ICTR was useful just because it has made Arusha known internationally, but it has also brought problems like the increase in the cost of living, rents of residential houses, and commodities. Another one talked about the positive effect of ICTR in creating employment, as well as the benefits to the government due to of its presence in the country. The *Arusha Times* itself wrote that "Come 2008, the UN Tribunal for Rwanda packs up to vacate Arusha. To some ordinary

---

[58]   The *Arusha Times*, ISSN 0856-6135, No 00330, July 24-30, 2004.

residents this could be a relief but to many organizations and businesses the going will be tough." The same newspaper[59] chose the following as its front-page headline: "AICC now braces for harder times. Centre lays off 92 employees in reform strategy." According to the managing director of AICC, interviewed by the newspaper, the ICTR contributes over 70% to their total income. The headquarter of ICTR is in their premises and some tribunal staff live in their residential facilities. So as a strategy to brace itself for difficult times ahead, AICC started its fiscal year 2004-2005 by laying off 92 employees, the newspaper said.

Another analysis[60] wondered if the local population understood what the end of the tribunal will mean socially and economically for Arusha residents. In this analysis, the then president of the ICTR staff association indicated that "apart from Tanzanians getting direct benefits, business in Arusha has also been boosted. The companies concerned range from petrol stations, insurance companies, post and telecommunication services, mobile phone companies, the tourism and travel industry, local and foreign super markets, banks, schools—especially international and those that use English as their main language—and public utility companies, to mention a few."

The developments above show the extent to which the presence of ICTR is perceived as having contributed to the development of the economy of Arusha. Of course, there are enormous benefits to the community that were not discussed, including the wide variety of travel tickets purchased by the ICTR from local travel agencies in Arusha. Actually, the organization bought tickets for its staff going on mission, for staff taking up their appointments in Arusha, for applicants invited for interviews, for staff leaving the duty station, for staff and dependents medically evacuated, for dependents on education grant travels, for staff and dependents on home leave and family visit travels, etc. This represents a huge benefit for travel companies. Another area which was

---

[59]   Ibid, ISSN 0856-6135; No 00332, August 7-13, 2004.
[60]   Nicodemus Ikonko in *Hirondelle*. 25.05.04 "ICTR/Economy—End of tribunal's mandate spells gloomy future for Arusha."

not covered due to the lack of accurate data was the DSA and travel for consultants and experts as well as the expenditures of visitors of ICTR and people coming to visit ICTR staff.

In the determination of the contribution of the ICTR, some assumptions were made which should be noted. The salary paid to local staff and the local portions paid to international staff were assumed to be spent in Arusha.

This study has only estimated the quantitative dimension of ICTR's impact on the Arusha economy. No attempt was made to ascertain the contribution on the human and cultural dimensions of the local life. The training programs organized by the ICTR for its local staff (language, computer, etc.), as well as the experience gained while working with the organization, represent benefits to the community as well as the country.

Overall, we can conclude that the ICTR made significant contributions to the local economy. These contributions include the creation of jobs and expenditures on goods and services. ICTR brings in revenues, which would otherwise not be generated in the community if it was not located in Arusha.

5.4   Recommendations

This section proposes general recommendations that could be of interest to the United Nations and the Tanzanian government, as well as the Arusha community.

5.4.1   Recommendations to the United Nations and ICTR

Incorporate into the mandate of the ICTR the responsibility of maximizing the value of the developmental impact of the organization's operations in Arusha in particular and in Tanzania in general. Currently, there is no one at the ICTR who is explicitly responsible for such an assignment. The idea of anticipating the impact of the closure of the ICTR appeared on the official agenda as a recommendation of the auditors.[61] Factoring into the decision-making process the need to contribute to the development of local businesses could achieve this recommendation.

This substantive concern could be addressed, at this late hour in the case of the ICTR by commissioning a comprehensive official study on the impact of its operations not only in Arusha but also in Rwanda, which is the primary target of the ICTR's main mission, rendering justice.

Maximizing the developmental impact of the international presence could also mean a bold commitment on the part of the ICTR to fill the huge gap between the present impact of its operations and the potential benefit to the local economy that could be generated by a development-driven approach in its activities. The hope would be to invert the trend discovered by this research, according to which close to 74.44% of the organization's expenditures are made outside Tanzania.

5.4.2 Recommendations to the Tanzanian Government and Local Stakeholders

Many opportunities have certainly been missed by the local businesses, since close to two-third of ICTR's overall expenses are made outside Tanzania. Had the government been more organized and proactive, more of the expenditures could have been made if not in Arusha, at least possibly in Tanzania. The ICTR budgetary submissions and allocations are reviewed by UN member states, including Tanzania. The availability of budgetary information allows the government and indirectly the business community to organize itself in order to capture

---

[61] A similar concern has arisen with regard to the peacekeeping, peace-building, or state-building operations entrusted to the United Nations as a whole.

a significant portion of the business opportunities offered by the ICTR procurement process.

The government and the appropriate stakeholders should organize themselves to minimize the negative economic impact of the anticipated winding up of ICTR operations in 2008-2010. The closure of the ICTR would probably entail direct job losses for Tanzanians employed by the ICTR and indirect jobs losses for those employed by ICTR staff members or businesses dependent on the presence of the ICTR. There will also be revenue losses for the Tanzanian government itself due to the disappearance/reduction of taxes indirectly paid by the ICTR through local businesses dependent on its presence. The AICC alone anticipates a loss of revenue of roughly $2,277,000 per year when the 10,000m² property rented by the ICTR will become vacant.

In a move to minimize the anticipated impact, the United Nations, in partnership with the Tanzanian government and other stakeholders (including the business community) should consider launching an initiative aimed at mapping out the most appropriate strategies and mobilizing the required resources for their smooth implementation. Some Arusha residents have initiated the thinking process and have a bag full of ideas aimed at helping the local government leaders to generate projects on "how to make the 'city' grow, even after (the) ICTR brothers and sisters have moved on."[62] They include:

1. Lobbying the United Nations to ensure that another UN or global outfit is established in Arusha to occupy the modern premises and infrastructure the ICTR will be leaving[63]
2. Ensuring that the East African Community scales up as the ICTR phases out by engaging the EAC bodies with enough issues to keep them busy and thus justify the residence in

---

[62] The *Arusha Times*, June 12-18, 2004.
[63] Are considered in this regard an "African Office" of the International Criminal Court; the headquarters of the African Court on Human and Peoples' Rights.

Arusha of members of the East African Legislative Assembly, judges of the East African Court of Justice, etc.

5.4.3   Recommendations for Further Research on the Topic

Undertaking a comprehensive and detailed study on the impact on the economy of the operations of the ICTR requires more time and resources than was available to us. Such a research remains to be carried out. Its success requires the official involvement of the ICTR itself to ensure the timely availability of first-hand and accurate information on the operations of the institution. Despite the support of the ICTR's management and interest shown by its officials in the outcome of the research, access to information remained a constant challenge. This was most of the time due to the heavy workload of the staff, the unavailability of the information needed, or the unwillingness to compute the data required, etc. Hence, it is important for the ICTR to accept this assignment as part of its overall social responsibility. Consequently, the proposed scope of the study should be expanded beyond Arusha to include Tanzania; beyond Tanzania to include Rwanda, where the ICTR has a big presence; and beyond economic impact to include other spheres of human activities—culture, health, social life, etc.

REFERENCES

Allison M. Ohme (2003) *The Economic Impact of a University on its Community and State:Examining Trends Four Years Later.* University of Delaware, Delaware, USA. Available at: http://www.udel.edu/ IR/Presentations/EconImpact.doc.

Grant Curtis (1993) "Transition to What? Cambodia UNTAC and the Peace Process". *United Nations Research Institute for Social Development (UNRISD) Discussion Paper*, Geneva. Availableat:ttp://.www.michiganrecycles.or/pdf/MRM Peconomics.pdf.

Krieger Douglas (2001) *Michigan Recycling Measurement Project: the Economic Impact of Recycling.* Michigan: Michigan Recycling Coalition

Jeffrey M. Humphreys, David G. Clements, Jo Anne Lowe, Tracie W. Sapp (1999) "Economic Impact of the University of Georgia in the Athens Area". *Georgia Business and Economic Conditions*, Vol 59, N0 3, Georgia: Terry College of Business.

Heater A. Kelly (2002) *The Economic Impact of the University of Delaware.* Newark: Office of Institutional Research and Planning, University of Delaware.

Ministry of Regional Administration and Local Government, Arusha Municipal Council (2004) *Socio-Economic Profile Year 2004.* Arusha: Arusha Municipal Council.

Paul Glewwe and Kwaku A. Twum-Baah (1991) "The Distribution of Welfare in Ghana, 1987-1988". Living Standards Measurement Study. Working Paper No. 75. Washington, D.C.: The World Bank.

UN Security Council establishing the ICT R (1994) *Resolution 955.* New York: United Nations.

Robert H. Baumann, David E. Dismukes, Dmitry V. Mesyanzhinov, Allan G. Pulsipher (2002) *Analysis of the Economic Impact Associated with Oil and Gas Activities on State Leases.* Baton Rouge: Louisiana State University Center for Energy Studies.

Ross B. Emmett, Varghese A. Manaloor (2000) *Augustana University College and the Camrose Area: An Economic Impact Study,* Camrose, Canada: Augustana University College. Available at: http://www. oit.montclair.edu.

S. Hussain Ali Jafri, Santhosh K. Durgam, D'Anna A. Jackson, Zeb Pomerenke (2004) *Economic Impact of Tarleton State University-Stephenville, Texas.* Stephenville: Tarleton State University.

The Arusha Times, No. 0001, No. 0062, No. 00322, No. 00324, No. 00330, No. 00332.

Uma Sekaran (2003) *Research Methods for Business. A skill Building Approach (4th Edition).* New York: John Wiley.

United Nations (1987) Secretariat Document/AI/343, 31 July 1987. New York: United Nations.

APPENDIX 1

QUESTIONNAIRE

Dear Participant,

This questionnaire is designed to collect information aimed at assessing and understanding the economic impact of the presence of the ICTR in the city of Arusha.

Because you are the one who can give me a correct picture of what you spend in Arusha, I kindly request your assistance in responding to the questions below frankly and honestly.

Thank you very much for your time and cooperation. I greatly appreciate your help in furthering this research endeavour.

Cordially,
Gloria Maxwell*

[Mobile phone: xxxx xxx xxx. Email: xxxxxx.xxx@gmail.com]

1. Do you employ Tanzanian Citizens (as house helps, gardeners, drivers, *askari*, etc.)?

   Yes [ ]   No [ ]

2. If "yes," how many in total?   _____

   House help: _____
   Gardener: _____
   Askari/Security guard: _____
   Driver: _____
   Other: _____

3. How much do you pay them per month?

    House help: _____
    Gardener: _____
    Askari/Security guard: _____
    Driver: _____
    Other: _____

4. How much do you pay as monthly rent? _____
5. How many cars do you own in Arusha? _____
6. How much (on average) do you spend in Arusha per month?

    a. Household (food, beverage, etc.): _____
    b. Medical expenses: _____
    c. TV subscription(s):_____ _____
    d. Telephone: _____
    e. Water: _____
    f. Electricity: _____
    g. Internet connection: _____
    h. Childcare & programs (after-school programs, sports, lessons, etc.): _____
    i. Car fuel consumption: _____
    j. Auto repairs: _____
    k. Souvenirs: _____
    l. Recreation (books, magazines, newspapers, audio CDs, DVDs, etc.): _____

7. Do you have children schooling in Arusha/Moshi?

    Yes [ ]   No [ ]

    If "Yes", how many? _____
    In which school(s) do they go? _____
    _____

8. Are you a client of "The Chissels. Arusha Duty Free"?

   Yes [ ]   No [ ]

   If "Yes," how much do you spend on average per month in the shop? _____

9. Voluntary Activities

   a. Have you been involved in any voluntary activities?
      Yes[ ] No [ ]
   b. Do you contribute financially to charitable activities or organizations? Yes [ ] No[ ]
   c. If "Yes", how much per year? _____

10. List other expenses you make per month in Arusha:

    a. _____
    b. _____
    c. _____

11. (For non-international staff only)

    Were you employed before joining the ICTR?

    Yes [ ] No [ ]

    If "Yes",
    a. In the private sector? _____
    b. Or in the civil service? _____
    c. How much was your monthly pay? _____
    d. How much do you currently earn monthly? _____

ABOUT THE AUTHORS

BONARD MWAPE

Bonard Mwape is a professor of public sector management. He is currently the director general of the Eastern and Southern African Management Institute (ESAMI) with its headquarters in Arusha, Tanzania. Previously, Professor Mwape was dean of students at the University of Zambia (UNZA), where he taught and conducted research for many years. He has more than twenty-five years of international experience and extensive practical experience in public service delivery, quick wins, strategic planning, institutional strengthening, capacity building, organisational system analysis, and development planning. Professor Mwape has strong knowledge and experience in managing international and multidisciplinary projects, particularly in the area of service delivery improvement, functional analysis, and institutional roles. At the ESAMI Business School, Professor Mwape supervises master's and doctoral research students and teaches many courses, including Policy Analysis, Strategic Management, Leading Change in Organizations, General Management, Organizational Behaviour, and Business Research Methods. Professor Mwape holds a PhD in public and international affairs from Pittsburgh University, USA, and an MSc degree in public administration and policy analysis from the University of London, UK.

Professor Mwape was born in Zambia, and he now lives with his family in Arusha. Arusha is a tourist hub perched on the slopes of Mount Meru in the northern tourist region of Tanzania, a few miles from Mount Kilimanjaro, the tallest mountain in Africa.

JOSEPH MUMBA

Joseph Mumba is an associate professor of management. He is currently the director of the ESAMI Business School at the Eastern and Southern African Management Institute, Arusha, Tanzania. Previously, Professor Mumba taught and researched physics and environmental technology at the University of Malawi for many years. He has more than twenty years of international experience in capacity building and consultancy in the areas of industrial environmental management, environmental assessment and audit, and energy management. At the ESAMI Business School, Professor Mumba supervises master's and doctoral research students and teaches many courses, including Business Research Methods, Business Mathematics and Statistics, Corporate Environmental Management, and Operations Management. Professor Mumba holds a PhD in mechanical engineering from Strathclyde University, Glasgow, Scotland, UK, and an MBA degree (Strategic Operations Management) from Prifysgol Cymru (University of Wales), Cardiff, Wales, UK.

Professor Mumba was born in Malawi and he now lives with his family in Arusha, Tanzania.

ABOUT THE BOOK

This book is designed as a thesis research manual for students pursuing policy research at a master's level. It is also intended for students completing master's in business administration (MBA) thesis and dissertation research projects.

The book is structured in a simple format that takes the student through the entire research process. It assumes a deductive research logic as a strategy to make business managers and policy implementers apply scientific thinking to solving business and policy problems.

The authors strongly believe that the book will make a big difference in the research lives of master's students in Africa and beyond. The complicated treatise on research found in many research methods books usually puts off average students. This book thus fills a big gap in readily available, affordable, and easily accessible simple research methods books to master's students in the developing world such as Africa and beyond.